CRIMINAL E-DISCOVERY
A Pocket Guide for Judges

SEAN BRODERICK
National Litigation Support Administrator
Administrative Office of the U.S. Courts, Defender Services Office

DONNA LEE ELM
Federal Defender
Middle District of Florida

JOHN HARIED
Co Chair, eDiscovery Working Group   EOUSA
U.S. Department of Justice

KIRAN RAJ
Senior Counsel to the Deputy Attorney General
U.S. Department of Justice

Federal Judicial Center
2015

This Federal Judicial Center publication was undertaken in furtherance of the Center's statutory mission to develop educational materials for the judicial branch. While the Center regards the content as responsible and valuable, it does not reflect policy or recommendations of the Board of the Federal Judicial Center.

first printing

Table of Contents

I. **Overview** 1
    A. Lack of Criminal e-Discovery Guidance 1
    B. Civil e-Discovery Rules and Practices Do Not Lend Themselves to Criminal e-Discovery............................. 2
    C. A Practitioner's Guide to Criminal e-Discovery............ 4

II. **Common Issues in Criminal e-Discovery** 5
    A. Funding the Defendant's e-Discovery............................ 5
    B. Lack of ESI Experience, Knowledge, and Competency 10
    C. Necessity of Litigation Support Assistance 11
    D. The Workflow in Processing ESI................................. 12
    E. Varieties of Evidence-Review Software 13
    F. Volume of e-Discovery 13
    G. Form of Production — ESI Formats 14
    H. Form of Production — Paper Formats 16
    I. Disorganized and Redundant ESI 17
    J. Providing Incarcerated Defendants Access to e-Discovery 17
    K. Multiple Defendants 18

III. **Judicial Management of Criminal e-Discovery** 19
    A. Managing Voluminous e-Discovery in Criminal Cases 19
    B. Early Discussion of e-Discovery Issues........................ 20
        Ask About the Case... 21
        Advise About Expectations 21
        Advise About Resources 22
        Schedule Discovery Conferences.............................. 22
    C. Subsequent Status of e-Discovery Issues..................... 22

IV. **Conclusion**... 23

Appendix A: ESI Protocol Description............................... 25
Appendix B: ESI Protocol 35
Appendix C: First Appearance e-Discovery Colloquy 73
Appendix D: Discovery Status Conference e-Discovery Colloquy 81

I. Overview

The rapid growth of digital technology and its spread into every facet of life are producing increasingly complex discovery issues in federal criminal cases. There are several advantages to electronically stored information (ESI, or e-discovery), including speed, efficiency, and quality of information. To ensure these benefits are realized, judges and lawyers working on federal criminal cases need guidance on how best to address e-discovery issues.

Judges can play a vital oversight role to ensure that e-discovery moves smoothly, trial deadlines are met, and the parties and courts are able to review and identify critical evidence. This pocket guide was developed to help judges manage complex e-discovery in criminal cases. A note of appreciation goes to Judge Xavier Rodriguez (W.D. Tex.), and Magistrate Judges Laurel Beeler (N.D. Cal.) and Jonathan W. Feldman (W.D.N.Y.), for their suggestions and advice, as well as to our fellow members of the Joint Electronic Technology Working Group, who improved this publication.

A. Lack of Criminal e-Discovery Guidance

Although the Federal Rules of Criminal Procedure offer guidance on a number of topics, they offer little help to judges and litigants concerning how to conduct e-discovery. As the Sixth Circuit noted in *United States v. Warshak*, Rule 16 of the Federal Rules of Criminal Procedure is "entirely silent on the issue of the form that discovery must take; it contains no indication that documents must be organized or indexed."[1] To be sure, Rule 16 provides a court the discretion to fashion discovery orders to serve the particular needs of a case, but it does not "specify the manner in which production is done."[2]

---

1. 631 F.3d 266, 296 (6th Cir. 2010). In that case, the defendant argued that the "district court must order the government to produce e ectronic discovery in a particu ar fashion." In rejecting this argument, the court noted that there is "a dearth of precedent suggesting that the district court was wrong" in a owing the government to produce discovery in an e ectronic format different from what the defendant sought. *Id.*

2. *See* Fed. Crim. Ru es Handbook § IV (Arraignment and Preparation for Tria) (Dec. 2012).

B. Civil e-Discovery Rules and Practices Do Not Lend Themselves to Criminal e-Discovery

The rules governing civil and criminal discovery are fundamentally dissimilar due to the different public policies underlying criminal and civil litigation, constitutional requirements, and special ethical obligations of prosecutors and defense counsel. Consequently, courts have generally refrained from applying civil e-discovery rules to criminal discovery.[3]

An essential difference between civil and criminal discovery is breadth:

> A criminal defendant is entitled to rather limited discovery, with no general right to obtain the statements of the Government's witnesses before they have testified. Fed. Rules Crim. Proc. 16(a)(2), 26.2. In a civil case, by contrast, a party is entitled as a general matter to discovery of any information sought if it appears "reasonably calculated to lead to the discovery of admissible evidence." Fed. Rule Civ. Proc. 26(b)(1).[4]

Federal Rule of Criminal Procedure 16 does not mandate any mechanisms or procedures for addressing e-discovery equivalent to those found in Federal Rules of Civil Procedure 26 and 34. Rule 16 includes "data" as a proper object of criminal discovery, but the rule does not address the mechanics of e-discovery.

Furthermore, the nature of the parties and proceedings differ in criminal cases. Unlike civil cases, where discovery is an adversarial process in which the government's discovery obligations are similar to any litigant's, the government has unique nonadversarial discovery obligations in criminal cases. As a representative of the sovereign, prosecutors are obliged to prosecute impartially and ensure that justice

---

3. The Sixth Circuit rejected the defendant's argument that the e ectronic discovery format standards of Federa Ru e of Civi Procedure 34(b)(2)(E)(i) shou d app y to crimina cases. *Warshak*, 631 F.3d at 296. Nonethe ess, two magistrate judges have turned to civi e-discovery ru es for guidance because there is a void in the crimina ru es regarding this issue. *See* United States v. O'Keefe, 537 F. Supp. 2d 14, 18 19 (D.D.C. 2008); United States v. Briggs, No. 10CR184S, 2011 WL 4017886, at *8 (W.D.N.Y. Sept. 8, 2011).

4. Degen v. United States, 517 U.S. 820, 825 26 (1996).

I. Overview

is done.[5] For example, the Due Process Clause imposes a "fundamental fairness" requirement on the government's discovery, as expressed in the government's *Brady* and *Giglio* obligations.[6] Additionally, speedy trial rights may be implicated when defendants have little time to come to grips with vast e-discovery.[7] Similarly, defendants are entitled to effective assistance of counsel at trial and during plea negotiations.[8] Defense counsel's effectiveness may depend on whether he or she has reviewed and understands the e-discovery in time to enter into informed plea negotiations.[9] When the government provides e-discovery in a reasonably organized fashion, it can help the defense efficiently review discovery and can lead to more productive plea discussions, less litigation, and speedier resolution of a case.

Criminal investigations and third-party subpoenas by both the prosecution and defense often bring vast quantities of ESI to criminal e-discovery. Complex ESI cases usually require litigation support resources not typically found in criminal defense practices. Indigent defendants need adequate funding to obtain those resources.

---

5. ABA Model Rules of Professional Responsibility 3.8, comt. 1; *see also* Berger v. United States, 295 U.S. 78 (1935).

6. *See also* United States v. Bagley, 473 U.S. 667, 675 (1985) (withholding *Brady* evidence violates due process). The prosecutor's *Brady* obligation is addressed in ABA Model Rule of Professional Conduct 3.8(d) (requiring prosecutors to "make timely disclosure to the defense of all evidence or information known to the prosecutor that tends to negate the guilt of the accused or mitigates the offense, and, in connection with sentencing, disclose to the defense and to the tribunal all unprivileged mitigating information known to the prosecutor, except when the prosecutor is relieved of this responsibility by a protective order of the tribunal.").

7. *See* U.S. Const. amend. VI; 18 U.S.C. § 3161 ("Speedy Trial Act").

8. Lafler v. Cooper, 132 S. Ct. 1376 (2012); Missouri v. Frye, 132 S. Ct. 1399 (2012).

9. Although lawyers need not review every document in a voluminous e-discovery production before entering into a plea bargain, they should review a reasonable and targeted portion of discovery so as to provide reasonably effective advice regarding resolution. Thus, depending upon the nature and complexity of the e-discovery, to conduct plea negotiations the defense may need to have e-discovery in a reasonably useable format, and have engaged in thoughtful e-discovery review.

Criminal e Discovery

C. A Practitioner's Guide to Criminal e-Discovery

One attempt to provide comprehensive, national guidance is the ESI Protocol (see Appendices A & B), which was produced by a joint working group composed of the Department of Justice and representatives of the criminal defense bar. [10] The ESI Protocol is one approach for judges to use to encourage interparty cooperation and reduce the need for judicial intervention. Indeed, some federal district courts have begun integrating the ESI Protocol into their courtroom practices.

The ESI Protocol draws on many sources, including case law, local rules, and seasoned defense and prosecution practitioners' experience. Its goal is to provide courts and litigants with best practices consisting of general principles, recommendations, and concrete strategies for improving efficiency, minimizing expense, increasing security, and decreasing frustration and litigation. Importantly, the ESI Protocol does not enlarge or diminish any party's substantive legal discovery obligations imposed by applicable federal statutes, rules, or case law. [2]

---

10. The Recommendations for E ectronica y Stored Information Discovery Production in Federa Crimina Cases (hereinafter "the ESI Protoco ") was produced by the Joint E ectronic Techno ogy Working Group (JETWG), which comprises representatives of the Administrative Office of the U.S. Courts (AOUSC), Defender Services Office (DSO), the Department of Justice (DOJ), Federa Pub ic and Community Defender Organizations (FPDOs and CDOs), private attorneys who accept Crimina Justice Act (CJA) appointments, and iaisons from the United States Judiciary and other AOUSC offices. The Federa Judicia Center does not endorse any specific discovery approach, inc uding the ESI Protoco .

11. *See, e.g.*, Best Practices for E ectronic Discovery in Crimina Cases: Western District of Washington (Mar. 21, 2013), *available at* http://www.wawd.uscourts.gov/sites/wawd/fi es/32113BESTPRACTICESFORELECTRONIC.pdf; Northern District of Ca ifornia, Crimina Justice Act, Capita and Non-Capita Crimina Representation (2001), *available at* http://www.cand.uscourts.gov/pages/965 (inking to the ESI Protoco).

12. *See, e.g.*, Brady v. Mary and, 373 U.S. 83 (1963); Gig io v. United States, 405 U.S. 150 (1972); 18 U.S.C. § 3500 (the "Jencks Act"); *and* Federa Ru es of Crimina Procedure 16 & 26.2.

4

II. Common Issues in Criminal e Discovery

The ESI Protocol will be familiar to most federal criminal practitioners. The Department of Justice trains its prosecutors to use the ESI Protocol in cases involving complex e-discovery. Most federal defenders and Criminal Justice Act (CJA) representatives receive similar training on the ESI Protocol.

II.   Common Issues in Criminal e-Discovery

Both prosecutors and defense attorneys struggle with the same e-discovery issues: large volume; a variety of sources and formats; hidden information (metadata and embedded data); differing formats for production; software and hardware limitations; and finding efficient, cost-effective ways to review ESI. Some challenges are unique to criminal practice, such as incarcerated defendants' access to e-discovery, while others are the same as those arising in civil practice. For many prosecutors and defense counsel, a lack of experience with ESI presents a significant challenge; but it is the lack of resources—money, personnel, training—that often overshadows all other problems. And even when resources are available, considerable time is often required to arrange for and execute the processing necessary to make ESI readily available.

For CJA counsel, the challenges of ESI may be especially daunting. Often, they are solo practitioners who lack the resources for sophisticated software tools. Because they are usually appointed post-indictment, they need to get up to speed on matters that the government may have spent many months or years investigating and preparing—while at the same time getting up to speed on how to manage electronic discovery. Besides training and software tools, they often may need experienced litigation support assistance, which can be provided pursuant to 18 U.S.C. § 3006A.

The following are e-discovery issues that judges may need to understand or address.

A.   Funding the Defendant's e-Discovery

There was a time when voluminous e-discovery cases were confined to white-collar prosecutions, and those defendants typically paid the costs of their own defense. Today, even routine drug cases and bank robberies often involve extensive cell phone data or other ESI. [3] This has funding consequences for indigent defendants and the court.

When a case has complex e-discovery issues, the judge considering a CJA appointment may need to factor in the additional cost of reviewing, organizing, and working with e-discovery. [4] The Act is silent about when a defendant would be so destitute as to need appointed counsel, but the cost of working with complex e-discovery can itself exceed what many defendants can afford even if they are able to pay for counsel. [5]

Some CJA panels have formal tiers or informal lists of specialized lawyers for capital, financial, or immigration cases. Courts that take their CJA attorneys' skills into consideration can also consider creating

---

13. Smartphone data provides an examp e of the magnitude of e-discovery. Many smartphones ho d sixteen to sixty-four gigabytes of data, not inc uding storage cards (which can doub e that amount), and have c oud access to much more data. They contain emai s, ca history and contact information, ca endars, text messages, GPS data, photographs, videos, internet history, and socia media information, a of which can resu t in thousands of potentia y re evant items of discovery. Mu ti-p e-defendant cases cou d dramatica y increase that amount. Add to that the corresponding aptops, tab ets, desktops, and survei ance data a so readi y accessib e, and the amount of e-discovery can quick y exceed document-based paper discovery in a white-co ar or corporate prosecution from fifteen years ago.

14. The court can ask the government to give it ear y notice if the case invo ves vo uminous e-discovery.

15. The Crimina Justice Act can authorize payment of e-discovery review costs when the extent of those costs wou d render a defendant unab e to pay for e-discovery review regard ess of whether a defendant can otherwise afford retained counse . 18 U.S.C. § 3006A(e)(1) a ows retained counse to app y for services to be paid through the CJA system. *See* Guide to Judiciary Po icies and Procedures, Vo . VII, § 310.10.20, *available at* http://www.uscourts.gov/ru es-po icies/judiciary-po icies/cja-guide ines/chapter-3-ss-310-genera #a310 10. If outside assistance is needed, the protoco for authorization and payment for investigative, expert, or other services in CJA-appointed cases is governed by Vo . VII, Chapter 3 of the Guide to Judiciary Po icies and Procedures. *See* http://www.uscourts.gov/Federa Courts/AppointmentOfCounse /CJAGuide inesForms/vo 7PartA/vo 7PartAChapter3.aspx. If counse anticipates that the costs wi exceed the statutory maximum, advance approva shou d be obtained from the court and the chief judge of the circuit (or the active or senior circuit judge who has been de egated authority to approve excess compensation). *See* Vo . VII, § 310.20.20 for further information and a samp e order, *available at* http://www.uscourts.gov/ru es-po icies/judiciary-po icies/cja-guide ines/chapter-3-ss-310-genera #a310 20.

II. Common Issues in Criminal e Discovery

a list of those lawyers who are proficient in e-discovery. [6] Although attorneys who lack familiarity with ESI will face a learning curve, experience with cases involving large amounts of ESI over time will develop a set of CJA lawyers readily capable of handling these cases.

In multidefendant cases, the court may be able to minimize costs by calling for cooperative sharing among defendants. This has been done for years whenever there is voluminous paper discovery, and many of those principles can apply to electronic discovery. One of the defense attorneys (often the federal defender) may take the lead for meet-and-confer discussions with the government regarding e-discovery productions and for distributing and providing basic organization of ESI when the defendants enter an agreement concerning discovery. The court can encourage centralizing e-discovery management and can approve a litigation support specialist, a technologist, or a paralegal working under that lawyer's supervision.

It also may be beneficial to place the discovery into a cloud-based document-review platform, [7] so defendants, counsel, investigators, and experts can access it as needed from various locations. Depending on what software different CJA lawyers have, all codefendants may not be able to use or take advantage of the same format of ESI production. [8] But any decision to rely on cloud-computing or reviewing services should include consideration of whether that service provider has provided adequate security to protect confidential, privileged, or oth-

---

16. On the other hand, courts must decide whether to expect a pane members to be prepared to hand e e-discovery on a arge sca e, given that every practitioner shou d deve op a base ine comfort with e-discovery. In August 2012, the ABA modified its ethics ru e on competency to inc ude fami iarity with techno ogy that may be used in representation. Comment 8 to Mode Ru e 1.1 provides: "To maintain the requisite know edge and ski , a awyer shou d keep abreast of changes in the aw and its practice, inc uding the *benefits and risks associated with relevant technology* . . . ." (emphasis added).

17. A document-review p atform uses a database and too s to capture, organize, ana yze, and review e-discovery. Whether stand-a one, networked, or in the c oud, these p atforms may enab e mu tip e individua s to secure y manage and access a arge amount of data.

18. By way of examp e and not as an endorsement of either App e computer systems or Microsoft Windows one common cha enge is that a number of CJA-pane attorneys use App e operating system ("Mac") computers, but App e systems work different y than the Windows computers that are standard with the DOJ and FDOs.

erwise sensitive e-discovery. [9] The Department of Justice and the defense bar expect to address criminal e-discovery security best practices in the near future, but in the interim, counsel should remain vigilant in protecting e-discovery.

Processing "raw" ESI into usable evidence that can be reviewed electronically is expensive and time-consuming.[20] As of 2015, in a relatively small case, processing five boxes (12,500 sheets) of paper business records costs approximately $4,800 and takes a trained DOJ litigation support professional employee three days. Similarly, processing twenty-five gigabytes of complex ESI costs approximately $3,200 and takes an employee two weeks.[2] Today, there is no software tool for producing all discovery in a single, easy-to-use package. Hopefully that will change as electronic discovery matures.

Fortunately, there are resources that can provide advice and guidance to judges about cost-effective means of managing e-discovery:

- The National Litigation Support Team (NLST), part of the Defender Services Office (DSO) of the Administrative Office of the U.S. Courts, is available to help attorneys for indigent defendants struggling with extensive e-discovery. The NLST writes recommendations for funding requests, advises courts and parties about economical and practical solutions to e-discovery issues, and provides direct assistance to lawyers.[22]

---

19. ESI protoco , Recommendation ¶ 10.

20. The term "processing" usua y invo ves formatting ESI so that the native fi e can be p aced into a review p atform where it can be viewed, cu ed, organized, searched, and ana yzed. For examp e, processing a native emai container fi e (a co - ection of emai s) invo ves extracting individua emai s and their attachments, whi e keeping track of the re ationship between the emai s and attachments, and converting the fi es to formats that can be read through a review too . For more information about processing raw ESI see *infra* section II.D.

21. The 2015 market rates for processing ESI range from $125 to $150 per gigabyte.

22. Before seeking court approva for any computer hardware or software with a cost exceeding $800, or for uti izing computer systems, itigation support products, services, or experts exceeding $10,000, appointed counse must consu t with the DSO for guidance. CJA counse must then inform the court in writing of the DSO's advice and recommendation regarding proposed expenditures. Guide to Judiciary Po icies and Procedures, vo . VII, § 320.70.40, *available at* http://www.uscourts.gov/

II. Common Issues in Criminal e-Discovery

The court can ask for assistance from the NLST.[23]

- The DSO has three national coordinating discovery attorneys (CDAs) who are experts in e-discovery, have experience with CJA cases, and are knowledgeable about litigation technology. They work with CJA counsel and federal defenders in multidefendant cases to manage large volumes of e-discovery efficiently and cost-effectively to best fit the defendants' needs. The court can ask CJA counsel to request that the case be referred to a CDA through the National Litigation Support Team.[24]

- All circuits except the Fifth, Eleventh, and D.C. have case budgeting attorneys (CBAs) who work with judges and CJA panel attorneys to develop and review budgets for criminal "mega cases."[25] They assist in addressing attorney and paralegal time, as well as expert, investigative, and other costs, to ensure that critical defense needs are budgeted to optimize resources while fostering high-quality, cost-controlled represen-

---

Federa Courts/AppointmentOfCounse /Viewer.aspx?doc /uscourts/Federa Courts/AppointmentOfCounse /vo 7/Vo 07.pdf.

23. The NLST can be contacted at (510) 637-3500. Further information about the NLST can be found on fd.org at http://www.fd.org/navigation/ itigation-sup port/subsections/who-is-the-nationa - itigation-support-team.

24. Further information regarding CDAs can be found on the J-Net at http://jnet.ao.dcn/court-services/cja-pane -attorneys-and-defenders/services-coordinating-discovery-attorneys-avai ab e-se ected-federa -crimina -justice-act-cases (not accessi-b e to the pub ic).

25. For CJA pane attorneys, "mega cases" are either: (a) federa capita prosecutions and capita habeas corpus cases, or (b) noncapita representations with the potentia for extraordinary cost (attorney work expected to exceed 300 hours or tota expenditures for attorneys and investigative, expert, and other service providers expected to exceed $30,000 for an individua CJA defendant). This is distinguished from "mega budget cases," referring to federa and community defender office cases that wi substantia y impact their office budgets (by a 10% or $500,000 increase or more), so that an additiona budget is deve oped to fund just that one case. *See Case Budgeting Techniques and Other Cost Containment Policies* (June 30, 2014), *available at* http://www.fd.org/docs/se ect-topics/cja/case-budgeting-techniques-and-other-cost-containment-strategies.pdf?sfvrsn 8.

tation. In appropriate cases, the budgets may address litigation support costs, and the CBAs have working relationships with the NLST to consult on litigation support matters. Judges in a district without a CBA can contact the DSO for assistance.[26]

There are considerable funding consequences to voluminous e-discovery. The court should expect additional CJA costs in these cases, but managing e-discovery can be done thoughtfully and reasonably to mitigate costs.

B. Lack of ESI Experience, Knowledge, and Competency

Unfortunately, many criminal practitioners still do not have an adequate understanding of e-discovery issues and litigation technology. However, attorney competency ethics standards are evolving to require an adequate understanding of e-discovery and the technology needed to review it.[27] Lawyers who are unfamiliar with e-discovery can associate or consult with others who have the expertise.[28] Nonetheless, they remain responsible for e-discovery decisions and should be able to do the following, either themselves or in association or consultation with others:

- Implement procedures to preserve potentially discoverable electronic information.

---

26. Further information on case budgeting and case budgeting attorneys can be found on the J-Net at http://jnet.ao.dcn/court-services/cja-pane-attorneys-and-defenders/case-budgeting (not accessib e to pub ic). Judges who do not have a CBA in their circuit can contact the duty attorney for the Defender Services Office at (800) 788-9908.

27. For examp e, the State Bar of Ca ifornia issued a forma ethics opinion on this subject in the summer of 2015. *See* State Bar of Ca . Standing Comm. on Prof' Responsibi ity and Conduct, Forma Op. No. 2015-193 (2015). This deve opment fo ows the 2012 American Bar Association amendment to its Mode Ru e 1.1, stating that awyers need to "keep abreast of changes in the aw and its practice, *including the benefits and risks associated with relevant technology.*" ABA Mode Ru es of Professiona Conduct, Mode Ru e 1.1, comt. 8 (emphasis added).

28. If a CJA attorney needs to retain expert assistance, payment wou d have to be approved by the court.

II. Common Issues in Criminal e Discovery

- Assess e-discovery needs and issues.
- Plan and perform appropriate searches.
- Understand how to manage, review, and produce e-discovery in a manner that preserves its integrity.

Because discoverable information is increasingly found and produced electronically, lawyers who are e-discovery illiterate may delay trial preparation. Technological "dinosaurs" may also miss potentially beneficial evidence, for example, by overlooking valuable metadata in electronic records because they are entrenched in printing their discovery. They also may make critical mistakes early in the case, inadvertently choosing production formats that they cannot use or that will not help find the evidence they need. When such mistakes result in not finding exculpatory evidence, they risk being ineffective.

The benefits of e-discovery can be lost on uninformed counsel. In making counsel appointments and resourcing cases, judges should be mindful that handling complex e-discovery cases requires an adequate understanding of ESI and available technology.

C. Necessity of Litigation Support Assistance

In any sizeable e-discovery case, finding appropriately skilled expert assistance is critical to reviewing the evidence and deciding whether to negotiate a plea agreement or take the case to trial. Individuals with litigation support expertise can be found in a variety of traditional job roles, working as paralegals, investigators, information technology (IT) specialists, computer technicians, data processors, software specialists, and more. Finding the correct fit of litigation support staff to the case early is a priority.

Litigation support specialists should have legal and IT experience and training to organize, analyze, and present case materials through technology equipment and computer programs. They should have the ability to harvest and extract electronic data and metadata from ESI; assist in meet-and-confer sessions regarding the exchange of ESI; monitor and manage discovery productions (both production and receipt); provide advice on how to search data; and manage the day-to-day operations of strategically collecting, processing, organizing, reviewing, analyzing, and presenting case data. Using both project management and technology, they ensure that e-discovery is handled in a cost-effective and time-efficient manner that allows for effective organization, easy retrieval, and quality client representation.

Just as judges should be mindful of attorney knowledge and experience in managing e-discovery, they should also be aware that even knowledgeable attorneys need skilled litigation support.

D. The Workflow in Processing ESI

ESI generally takes one of two possible forms: preprocessed (raw) or postprocessed. Some raw ESI is not ready to be reviewed electronically; it must be processed[29] into a digital file that can be loaded into document-review software. Similarly, paper records can be processed into electronic files like TIFFs with extracted text or searchable PDFs with the extracted text embedded in the file itself.

The workflow for processing ESI can be complicated. When ESI is in a proprietary format (for example, a Google Mail file), it cannot be reviewed with industry-standard tools; instead, review requires specialized hardware, software, and expertise to convert the data into a form that can be reviewed with standard tools.[30] Even if the discovery is produced in an optimal way,[3] defense counsel may still need expert assistance, such as litigation support personnel, paralegals, or database vendors, to convert e-discovery into a format they can use and to decide what processing, software, and expertise is needed to assess the ESI. Next, the ESI should be organized to facilitate finding informa-

---

29. *See supra* n. 20 for a definition of "processing."

30. Many state and federa aw enforcement agencies have outdated computer systems, so the data in these outdated systems cannot be viewed with current industry-standard itigation support software. This is particu ar y common with audio and video fi es, necessitating conversion to industry-standard formats.

31. Parties shou d not be obstructionist and ought to produce discovery in a usab e format if they reasonab y can. According to the ESI Protoco , when a producing party e ects to engage in processing ESI, the resu ts of that processing (un ess it contains work product) shou d be produced as discovery; this saves the receiving party the expense of rep icating the work. ESI Protoco , Recommendations ¶ 6(d). That said, the ESI Protoco states that the government is not ob igated to convert ESI into a format specified by the defense beyond what it wou d do for its own case preparation or discovery production.

II. Common Issues in Criminal e Discovery

tion. In voluminous e-discovery cases, parties must be able to rely on document-review software, which can be costly. Nonetheless, it saves money because it speeds up the review process and improves counsel's ability to find information. Such software affords counsel a variety of search strategies, including word searches, document searches, date searches, sender/recipient searches, concept searches, and predictive coding searches.[32]

E. Varieties of Evidence-Review Software

There is a vast array of software tools for handling all of the stages of electronic discovery: preserving, collecting, and harvesting data; processing and/or converting ESI; searching and retrieving information; reviewing ESI; and presenting evidence. There is frequently overlap between what various products can do. No single software tool does everything needed for e-discovery. Some tools specialize in processing raw ESI into formats that another tool can then use, while other tools specialize in a discrete function such as document review, strategic analysis, case organization, production of discovery, or evidence display in the courtroom. As a result, litigants have different collections of tools. That creates compatibility and conversion issues.

A meet-and-confer is an important stage in tackling those compatibility and conversion issues, particularly when the parties do not already have an established routine for exchanging discovery or when they face novel or difficult ESI issues. One goal of the meet-and-confer is to address technical issues so that the ESI produced in discovery is readable and usable. An important part of that process is the parties' discussion of production formats, volume, timing, and other issues.[33]

F. Volume of e-Discovery

The great volume of e-discovery poses a serious challenge due to the variety of devices on which ESI can be created and stored, the ease of

---

32. Techno ogy-assisted review (a so ca ed predictive coding) is a process for prioritizing or coding a co ection of documents using a computerized system that the harnesses human judgments of one or more subject matter expert(s) on a sma er set of documents, and then extrapo ates those judgments to the remaining data.

33. *See* ESI Protoco , attached as Appendix B.

various forms of telecommunication (such as texting and social media), and the declining cost of storage. ESI can come from many custodians[34] or sources—mobile phones, smartphones, tablets, laptops, desktops, computer network servers, external ESI storage devices (such as flash drives or external hard drives), cloud storage, GPS tracking devices, social media. Because of this, the amount of ESI in criminal cases has grown exponentially, and this growth is expected to continue, significantly complicating management and review of evidence. For example, in 2011, court-appointed defense counsel in one multi-defendant case had to review discovery comprising 240,000 pages of documents on 19 DVDs and CD ROMS, 185 banker boxes of paper documents (approximately 460,000 pages), and 30 forensic images (that is, copies) of complete computers, servers, and thumb drives holding approximately 4.3 terabytes of data.[35] Additionally, the defendants gathered 750,000 pages of third-party information directly relevant to their defenses. Cases like this benefit substantially from sophisticated software and advanced review practices such as technology-assisted review.

It is important to recognize that complex ESI requiring technological assistance is not constrained to computer and white-collar fraud crimes. Vast amounts of ESI are found in small cases as well. Even relatively modest amounts of e-discovery, depending on format, can create obstacles to reviewing evidence. Moreover, simple cases of possession of drugs or guns, for example, can involve smartphones and computers containing gigabytes or even terabytes of data. Lawyers unaided by technology cannot review this much data.

G. Form of Production—ESI Formats

The format in which ESI is gathered affects how the data can be used. For example, text messages collected as text-only files can be searched for particular words or combinations of words. But if the metadata for those same text messages is also gathered, then thousands or millions of text messages can not only be searched for particular words, they

---

34. In e-discovery terms, "custodian" refers to the person whose data was co - ected.

35. App ying itigation support standard ca cu ations, 4.3 terabytes of data is the equiva ent of 215 mi ion pages, or 86,000 banker boxes, of documents.

II. Common Issues in Criminal e-Discovery

can also be sorted by date, custodian, and author or addressee, and software can plot who communicated with whom, how frequently, when, and where. Such information can have tremendous utility in criminal cases.

Lawyers need specialized litigation software to work with ESI in its many formats. For example, they need software to review ESI documents, which can be as basic as a PDF viewer or far more complex. Most document-review platforms allow parties to view many file types. The DOJ and most civil law firms have managed their own discovery materials with software programs and technical personnel for years. Criminal defense practitioners, especially those involved in indigent defense, are relative latecomers to this world. Most CJA panel attorneys do not have litigation support software that can view and organize TIFF or native file productions. Similarly, most do not have tools to take advantage of a "load file,"[36] extracted metadata, or files in native or near-native ESI format.[37] It is only recently that federal defender offices gained that capability nationally. As a result, the DOJ may be able to produce discovery in a reasonably usable format, but CJA counsel may not be able to utilize the most robust litigation software available. To provide computer-challenged defense counsel with reasonably useable e-discovery, the U.S. Attorney's Office typically provides e-discovery on disks that contain software for viewing, searching, and tagging documents. For more sophisticated defense counsel, the DOJ typically creates load files or otherwise configures its e-discovery productions in industry-standard formats. Of course, there are instances where typical practices do not work well, and those are proper subjects for a meet-and-confer.

To benefit from the information available in e-discovery, attorneys must know what format the original data was in, what formatting options are available, and how those options affect their potential review

---

36. A load file is a cross-reference file used to import images or data into databases. A data load file may contain Bates numbers, metadata, paths to native files, coded data, and extracted or OCR text. An image load file may contain document-boundary, image-type, and path information. Load files must be obtained and provided in software-specific formats to ensure they can be used by the receiving party.

37. A significant advantage to web-hosted document-review platforms for the CJA panel is that IT support is provided by the vendor, since most do not have in-house IT staff.

of the data. Attorneys who do not understand the various formats should consult with a litigation support or IT expert before receiving or processing their e-discovery.

H. Form of Production—Paper Formats

Some contemporary records and many historical records only exist on paper. Converting paper discovery to electronic formats makes it easier to duplicate, exchange, and search. But converting voluminous paper records takes time and money. Accurate document breaks (also known as document unitization[38]) too frequently are not captured when scanning paper records. When this happens, document unitization is lost, diminishing the utility of the resulting electronic files. Although the producing party is not obligated to reformat paper records into an electronic form,[39] in some cases both parties may save time and money by converting paper into electronic formats. Cost sharing may be an option if the parties agree that scanning serves both sides.

Scanning a paper record and making it searchable through optical character recognition (OCR) software is an improvement over leaving it in paper form, but it is not a perfect solution. Scanning can be prohibitively expensive. Moreover, OCR programs have established error rates, decreasing the accuracy and reliability of electronic searches of documents. That unreliability causes some attorneys to default to using their own eyes to search rather than scanning paper records for electronic review.

Today, some records custodians' systems still are configured to produce subpoenaed records in paper, even when they have the same data electronically. If a records custodian is willing to produce the information in an electronic format, the electronic version usually will yield more reliable searches.[40] However, what is efficient and afforda-

---

38. Document unitization is the process of determining where a document begins (its first page) and ends (its ast page), with the goa of accurate y describing what was a "unit" as it was received by the party or was kept in the ordinary course of business by the document's custodian.

39. *See* ESI Protoco , Princip e 6.

40. There are severa options for e ectronic formats. Sometimes the records custodian can produce the native-format version, for examp e, a Word document as a Word fi e as opposed to a paper document or a PDF. Sometimes the native format

II. Common Issues in Criminal e Discovery

ble for records custodians, and what electronic formats they are willing or able to produce, varies widely.

I. Disorganized and Redundant ESI

E-discovery can come from records custodians as a disorganized and redundant jumble. That sometimes arises from how custodians store their data: multiple versions of the same computer record may coexist in unrelated computer systems, especially with cloud computing. Custodians may not be aware that copies of files exist in different parts of their system since files are often copied or backed up automatically without user interaction. With the ease of web communication, the multitude of different mobile devices, and inexpensive storage, ESI is frequently copied, recopied, forwarded, backed up, and archived many times over, resulting in multiple copies of the same files. Unlike paper records, where information was actively managed by records custodians who culled records to save money, there is often little need to organize ESI and delete duplicates or drafts. Although no single software quickly solves the issue of disorganized and redundant ESI, there are workflow processes combined with different types of software that can assist counsel in reducing duplicates, organizing the materials, and identifying the most relevant information more quickly than having a human look at every page.

J. Providing Incarcerated Defendants Access to e-Discovery

Defendants in pretrial detention face significant e-discovery challenges. Their rights to assist in their defense and confront the evidence against them contemplate reviewing that evidence. When out of custody, they can use their own (or their attorney's) computers to review electronic

---

is proprietary, and requires a proprietary viewer. Many video recording systems are proprietary. In some instances, a records custodian can produce a "near-native" version. For examp e, Goog e Mai (Gmai) is a web-based emai system. For production, a Gmai fi e can be converted to an .msg fi e format that can be readi y viewed. A ternative y, a document can be produced as an e ectronic TIFF image with extracted text that can be oaded into a database and e ectronica y searched. Or documents can be converted to a searchab e Adobe PDF format.

17

discovery. When detained, their access to computers often is very limited. Although jails have long had policies for managing inmates' paper discovery, most do not have policies allowing inmates to review electronic discovery. Moreover, when the detention facilities do not have computers readily available for inmate evidence review, acceptable equipment and software must be purchased for incarcerated defendants to use. Although defender offices are budgeted for such equipment, CJA attorneys may need the court to fund equipment purchases or rentals.

Providing defendants in-custody access to technology that allows them to review their e-discovery reduces attorney time and costs. When incarcerated defendants cannot review e-discovery on their own time, the attorney or investigator has to bring a laptop or tablet containing the e-discovery to a jail visit and maintain control of the device while allowing the defendant to review the evidence, resulting in many hours of time billed to the CJA appropriations. Additionally, defendants may be able to locate critical evidence much more quickly than defense team members who are unfamiliar with the documentation. By reviewing and discussing evidence early, defendants help their counsel prioritize the investigation and limit the data that must be reviewed. This also creates more meaningful meetings, allowing both counsel and defendant to make timely decisions.

Jails have legitimate security and staffing interests in preventing inmates from having unfettered access to computers. A joint DOJ and defense attorney working group is studying the risks and benefits of allowing inmates access to computers for e-discovery review. They hope to produce practical recommendations. In the interim, consultation between the government, the defense, and the particular facility is most likely to result in an acceptable solution.

K. Multiple Defendants

Multidefendant, high-volume e-discovery cases are fertile ground for generating discovery disputes that require a judge's attention. For example, fraud cases involving multiple defendants may include millions of pages of documents. Multiple-defendant drug cases tend to have fewer documents, but they typically make up for that with wiretaps, surveillance photos and videos, text messages, GPS data, and social media. These discovery items cannot be readily searched for defendant-specific materials without the use of litigation technology software. Even with software, it can take considerable time to review and analyze such complex and voluminous information.

With so many variables in play, multidefendant prosecutions may develop more conflicts over discovery than single-defendant prosecutions. One attorney may request additional information about the alleged criminal enterprise to receive more context about the case, while another may request different forms of production. Defense counsel may disagree with each other about formats of production, how the evidence is indexed and organized, and what information they are searching for. Prosecutors can find themselves caught in the middle of these competing demands and may not be able, or may not believe it is reasonable or affordable, to agree to varying (and potentially conflicting) defense counsel requests. This situation is ripe for pretrial e-discovery disputes. Judges can encourage the parties to attempt to resolve disputes without resorting to motion practice but may still be called upon to adjudicate competing discovery interests, especially where the government is subject to conflicting requests.

III. Judicial Management of Criminal e-Discovery

A. Managing Voluminous e-Discovery in Criminal Cases

As discussed earlier, voluminous e-discovery cases present difficult challenges for prosecutors and defense counsel. Depending upon the lawyers' familiarity with e-discovery, the court may need to exercise oversight in such cases. The ESI Protocol addresses the most common e-discovery issues, and the court can direct the parties to the ESI Protocol for guidance. Often, e-discovery disputes are simply the result of the lawyers' inexperience with e-discovery or their misunderstanding of technical terminology. Knowing that the lawyers are knowledgeable about e-discovery and/or that they have qualified litigation support, IT, or paralegal assistance will be of great assistance to judges managing these cases.

One key to success with these cases is addressing e-discovery issues early. Missteps at the outset of the case are costly to unwind or correct, and they waste time and money. To get the parties to address e-discovery issues early, the ESI Protocol recommends three steps:

1. At the outset of the case, the parties should meet and confer about the nature, volume, and mechanics of producing e-discovery.[4]

2. At the meet-and-confer, the parties should address what is being produced; a table of contents; the forms of production; volume; software and hardware limitations; inspection of seized hardware; and a reasonable schedule for producing e-discovery.[42]

3. The producing party transmits its e-discovery in sufficient time to permit reasonable management and review, and the receiving party should be proactive about testing the accessibility of the ESI when it is received.[43]

Although the Federal Rules of Criminal Procedure do not specify when evidence must be produced, some judges find it useful to have standing orders that direct the parties to come up with a discovery plan when dealing with complex e-discovery matters.

To get the parties started on the right foot, the court may want to address the topic of e-discovery at one of the initial hearings, even before the parties have conducted their first meet-and-confer session. A discovery status conference can be scheduled after the meet-and-confer takes place. Proposed colloquies are offered in Appendices C and D.

B. Early Discussion of e-Discovery Issues

There are four steps courts can take early on in a large e-discovery criminal case. First, the court can ask the parties questions to ascertain what issues they are facing. Second, the court can be clear about its expectations for parties handling voluminous e-discovery. Third, the

---

41. ESI Protoco , Recommendations ¶ 5.
42. ESI Protoco , Strategies ¶ 5.
43. ESI Protoco , Strategies ¶ 5(o).

III. Judicial Management of Criminal e Discovery

court can advise the parties of resources available to assist them. Finally, the court can schedule a discovery status conference as needed.

Ask About the Case: Appendix C offers a sample colloquy for the first appearance in the case. The court can ask the government the threshold question of whether this is a case in which the volume and/or nature of the e-discovery significantly increases the complexity of the case. In cases with court-appointed counsel, the answer may help the court decide whom to appoint and what resources and assistance appointed counsel may need.[44] Once both parties appear, the court can ask whether the parties have already addressed e-discovery issues, as that may obviate the need for further court involvement. The court can further ask if the parties are familiar with the ESI Protocol; if not, the prosecutor can provide a copy to defense counsel.

Advise About Expectations: Given the varying levels of experience and comfort with e-discovery and technology, as well as the rapid evolution of litigation software, the court can make clear from the outset its expectations for the lawyers in a complex e-discovery case.

Appendix C sets forth a list of reasonable expectations for the lawyers. These include the following:

- The lawyers should have an adequate understanding of e-discovery such that they can identify, communicate on, and solve common e-discovery problems and determine what forms of production are possible, how different software products and services can assist in the particular case, and what costs and cost savings result from their choices. The lawyers should be sufficiently familiar with the capabilities and limitations of software and services in order to select appropriate software and outside assistance. Lawyers can, of course, rely on experts to consult and advise them on what programs to use and what staff to retain.

---

44. *See* section II.A, *supra*, regarding funding e ectronic discovery.

- Although the court will encourage parties to obtain technical assistance, the lawyers are ultimately responsible for decisions involving e-discovery.
- The parties will meet and confer once they have secured expert assistance. A meet-and-confer discussion should occur well before any discovery status conference. When appropriate, the lawyers should bring experts with them to the meet-and-confer to address the technical aspects of e-discovery.

Advise About Resources: Public defenders and CJA counsel in multidefendant, complex e-discovery cases can petition the court to appoint a coordinating discovery attorney. If the court appointed counsel (either an assistant federal defender or a CJA panel attorney), counsel can contact the NLST for assistance.[45]

Schedule Discovery Conferences: Complex e-discovery cases may benefit from one or more discovery conferences, as the court deems appropriate.

C. Subsequent Status of e-Discovery Issues

Appendix D has a proposed colloquy for discovery status conferences. If status conferences are held, the judge can check on the progress of e-discovery. Depending on what the parties report has transpired since the last proceeding, the judge may remind them of the court's expectations as well as remind them of the resources available to them. Additionally, particular issues may arise that should be addressed in-depth.

Despite strong encouragement from the bench and the best intentions of the parties, the lawyers may not have conducted a meaningful meet-and-confer session. The Seventh Circuit's civil e-discovery pilot project revealed that many litigants are not diligent about conducting effective meet-and-confer sessions.[46] Even if meetings take place, if inexperienced lawyers did not bring expert assistance, or did not address

---

45. *See* section II.A, *supra*, for further discussion of the Defender Services Office's Nationa Litigation Support program.

46. Seventh Circuit E ectronic Discovery Pi ot Program: Fina Report on Phase Two 77, *available at* http://www.discoverypi ot.com/sites/defau t/fi es/Phase-Two-Fina -Report-Appendix.pdf.

IV. Conclusion

the matters in any depth (a so-called drive-by meet-and-confer), then problems with e-discovery may not have been avoided. Although not every case or lawyer needs these formal meetings, the court can satisfy itself that the parties have worked together to ensure productive access to e-discovery.

At the discovery status conference, the lawyers should provide a discovery disclosure schedule. The judge can clarify what is expected in continued "rolling" discovery, and that disclosure should take place expeditiously, since reviewing e-discovery can be very time-intensive. The court should take this opportunity to advise the parties about their discovery obligations. If the defense will have e-discovery, the court can check if the parties discussed that in the meet-and-confer session; if not, it could order a second meet-and-confer session.

There may be e-discovery issues that the parties have identified but have not been able to solve. If satisfied that they have tried in good faith to settle the matters first, the court can either decide the discovery dispute impromptu, or it can schedule a briefing and a discovery hearing. Subsequent discovery status conferences can be scheduled as needed.

IV.   Conclusion

The purpose of this guide is to help judges give guidance and direction to lawyers handling complex criminal electronic discovery. It aims to ensure that the parties manage the case efficiently and thoughtfully, avoid unnecessary delay and costs occasioned by the nature of the e-discovery, and provide defendants full access to the evidence necessary to evaluate the case and make strategic decisions. Of course, this guide cannot answer every e-discovery question that will arise, so judges must be creative in dealing with the myriad of issues that naturally arise in this dynamic field. But this guide does offer an overall framework for addressing criminal e-discovery that can be adapted to virtually every case.

Judges using this publication are encouraged to comment and propose changes to keep it current and relevant.

Appendix A
ESI Protocol Description

Appendix A: ESI Protocol Description

A. ESI Protocol Helps Judges with e-Discovery in Criminal Cases

The ESI Protocol provides practical recommendations to facilitate electronic evidence discovery (e-discovery or ESI) in criminal cases. It seeks to increase efficiency, save money, and reduce litigation over e-discovery issues. To accomplish these goals, the ESI Protocol creates a predictable framework for e-discovery discussions and production, and encourages the parties to resolve e-discovery disputes without court intervention. It was designed to be enduring and flexible by providing both broad principles that will apply regardless of technical changes and detailed guidance that can be updated as technology evolves.

The ESI Protocol has four parts:

1. **Principles:** The 10 Principles are core tenets that set the framework for the recommendations and strategies, and they also serve as a starting place for the uninitiated. A judge can direct a lawyer to begin by reviewing the principles.

2. **Recommendations:** The 10 Recommendations address critical e-discovery topics at a policy level. They are based upon the principles' core tenets, and they are intended to endure inevitable changes in technology. The recommendations are a framework for informed discussions between the parties about e-discovery issues.

3. **Strategies and Commentary:** The strategies and commentary section addresses the same topics as the 10 Recommendations. It provides practical guidance on key practices. The strategies and commentary will evolve over time in response to changing technology and experience. This section concludes with definitions of e-discovery terms.

4. **Checklist:** This one-page checklist for lawyers and judges identifies the major specific topics to address at a meet-and-confer conference or discovery hearing.

B. Overview of the ESI Protocol

Guiding principles. The ESI Protocol is built upon ten principles:

Principle 1:

    Lawyers have a responsibility to have an adequate understanding of electronic discovery.

Principle 2:

    In the process of planning, producing, and resolving disputes about ESI discovery, the parties should include individuals with sufficient technical knowledge and experience regarding ESI.

Principle 3:

    At the outset of a case, the parties should meet and confer about the nature, volume, and mechanics of producing ESI discovery. Where the ESI discovery is particularly complex or produced on a rolling basis, an ongoing dialogue may be helpful.

Principle 4:

    The parties should discuss what formats of production are possible and appropriate, and what formats can be generated. Any format selected for producing discovery should maintain the ESI's integrity, allow for reasonable usability, reasonably limit costs, and, if possible, conform to industry standards for the format.

Principle 5:

    When producing ESI discovery, a party should not be required to take on substantial additional processing or format-conversion costs and burdens beyond what the party has already done or

Appendix A: ESI Protocol Description

would do for its own case preparation or discovery production.

Principle 6:

Following the meet-and-confer, the parties should notify the court of ESI discovery production issues or problems that they reasonably anticipate will significantly affect the handling of the case.

Principle 7:

The parties should discuss ESI discovery transmission methods and media that promote efficiency, security, and reduced costs. The producing party should provide a general description and maintain a record of what was transmitted.

Principle 8:

In multidefendant cases, the defendants should authorize one or more counsel to act as the discovery coordinator(s) or seek appointment of a coordinating discovery attorney.

Principle 9:

The parties should make good faith efforts to discuss and resolve disputes over ESI discovery, involving those with the requisite technical knowledge when necessary, and they should consult with a supervisor, or obtain supervisory authorization, before seeking judicial resolution of an ESI discovery dispute or alleging misconduct, abuse, or neglect concerning the production of ESI.

Principle 10:

> All parties should limit dissemination of ESI discovery to members of their litigation team who need and are approved for access, and they should also take reasonable and appropriate measures to secure ESI discovery against unauthorized access or disclosure.

Scope. The ESI Protocol is intended only for cases in which the volume and/or nature of the ESI produced as discovery significantly increases the complexity of the case.[47] For example, cases involving a large volume of ESI, unique ESI issues, or multiple defendants may benefit from using the ESI Protocol. In simple or routine cases,[48] the parties should provide discovery in the manner they deem most efficient in accordance with the Federal Rules of Criminal Procedure, local rules, and custom and practice within their district.[49]

Limitations. The ESI Protocol does not alter the parties' discovery obligations or protections under the U.S. Constitution, the Federal Rules of Criminal Procedure, the Jencks Act, other statutes, case law (for example, *Brady* and *Giglio*), or local rules.[50] It is not intended to serve as a basis for allegations of misconduct or claims for relief, nor does it create any rights or privileges for any party.[5] Cases involving classified information have their own unique legal procedures that do not fit within the ESI Protocol.[52] The ESI Protocol applies only to postindictment criminal discovery, not civil litigation or preindictment investigations, both of which are governed by existing legal standards.[53]

An integrated process, not rules to be enforced. The ESI Protocol envisions a collaborative approach to e-discovery based upon

---

47. ESI that is contraband (*e.g.*, chi d pornography) requires specia discovery procedures. *See* ESI Protoco , Recommendations at 2.
48. Even sma amounts of ESI in an unusua or difficu t format can increase the comp exity of e-discovery, which wou d counse using the ESI Protoco .
49. See ESI Protoco , Recommendations ¶ 2.
50. ESI Protoco , Recommendations ¶ 3.
51. *Id.*
52. ESI Protoco , Recommendations ¶ 5.
53. ESI Protoco , Recommendations, fn. 1.

Appendix A: ESI Protocol Description

the mutual and interdependent responsibilities of the opposing parties.[54] As such, the ESI Protocol sets forth best practices for litigants, not a set of enforceable rules.

Balancing competing goals. As with the criminal discovery rules, the ESI Protocol seeks to balance competing goals. For example, to promote cost savings, the ESI Protocol states that if the producing party elects to process ESI for its own case preparation or discovery production, then the results of that processing should—unless they constitute work product—be produced in discovery to save the receiving party the expense of replicating that work. An illustration would be that if the producing party scans paper documents to a TIFF image and OCR text, then those should be provided in discovery rather than providing only the paper documents. Nonetheless, the producing party's work product—for example, issue tags or document notes—should not be produced. Importantly, the producing party should not be required to take on substantial additional processing or format-conversion costs and burdens beyond what it has already done or would do for its own case preparation or discovery production.

No easy solutions. A natural human tendency when confronted with complex problems is to look for easy solutions. But the ESI Protocol recognizes that at this point in the evolution of e-discovery, there is no easy, one-size-fits-all solution.

Coordinating discovery for multiple defendants. In multiple-defendant cases, the ESI Protocol recommends that the defendants authorize one or more defense counsel to act as the discovery coordinator or seek the appointment of a coordinating discovery attorney (CDA). CDAs are Defender Services Program–contracted attorneys who have technological knowledge and experience, resources, and staff to assist with the effective management of complex e-discovery.[55]

Communication, not litigation. To reduce costs and save time, the ESI Protocol avoids a purely adversarial and rules-driven approach to e-discovery. First, the ESI Protocol recommends that the parties meet and confer at the outset of a case. Second, it recommends

---

54. *See* ESI Protoco , Introduction at 2.
55. For more information on coordinating discovery attorneys, see section III.A, *supra*, at pp. 14 15.

communication as a precondition to filing a motion about an e-discovery issue. An aggrieved party is directed to confer with opposing counsel in a good-faith effort to resolve the dispute, and to involve individuals with sufficient knowledge to understand the technical issues, or sufficient authority to settle the dispute cooperatively, before filing any motions. If a motion is filed, the ESI Protocol suggests including a statement of counsel for the moving party stating that, after consultation with the opposing party, they have been unable to resolve the dispute without court action.

Each U.S. Attorney's Office and Main Justice criminal component has one or more criminal discovery coordinators who are responsible for providing guidance to prosecutors on criminal discovery topics. Each federal and community defender office has IT or other staff and access to the National Litigation Support Team that can provide technical assistance in resolving discovery issues. Lawyers can take advantage of these resources to understand technical issues and facilitate meaningful discussion that may avoid or resolve conflicts.

To avoid unnecessary motions practice, the ESI Protocol calls for supervisor participation in resolving disputes and recommends that prosecutors and federal and community defender offices institute internal procedures that require line prosecutors and defenders to: (1) seek a supervisor's assistance in resolving an e-discovery dispute, (2) consult with supervisors before filing motions seeking judicial resolution of an e-discovery dispute; and (3) obtain a supervisor's authorization before alleging that opposing counsel has engaged in any misconduct, abuse, or neglect concerning the production of ESI. These recommendations were included to ensure that the parties explored technological and pragmatic solutions before resorting to e-discovery litigation. Of course, the recommendations for consulting with, or obtaining approval of, a supervisor do not apply to CJA or privately retained counsel.

Whether the ESI Protocol's meet-and-confer approach will succeed in our adversarial system will depend in some measure upon whether judges encourage the parties to follow the ESI Protocol. At the least, the involvement of technically knowledgeable personnel should help to avoid disputes based on technological misunderstandings.

Appendix A: ESI Protocol Description

Parties are responsible for identifying and solving e-discovery issues. The ESI Protocol identifies the responsibilities of both parties. Some examples follow.

Both Parties
- When gathering ESI, think about the nature, volume, and mechanics of managing ESI.[56]
- Conduct a meet-and-confer to discuss e-discovery issues, and address eighteen specified topics as necessary.[57] Use the one-page checklist to help identify possible issues.
- Discuss any issues concerning information provided in discovery that implicates any privilege or that is protected as confidential or personal identifying information.[58]
- Discuss a reasonable schedule for producing e-discovery.[59]
- Discuss e-discovery security if either party intends to make discovery electronically available to others.[60]
- Discuss protective orders if needed.[6]
- Memorialize any e-discovery agreements.[62]
- Give the court advance notice of any issues that will significantly affect the production or review of e-discovery, the need to request supplemental funds, or the scheduling of pretrial motions or trial.[63]

---

56. ESI Protoco , Strategies ¶ 2.
57. ESI Protoco , Strategies ¶ 5.
58. ESI Protoco , Strategies ¶ 5(e).
59. ESI Protoco , Strategies ¶ 5(o).
60. ESI Protoco , Strategies ¶ 5(p).
61. ESI Protoco , Strategies ¶ 5(q).
62. ESI Protoco , Strategies ¶ 5(r).
63. ESI Protoco , Strategies ¶ 5(s).

Producing Party
- When possible, produce ESI as processed to save the receiving party the expense of replicating the processing.[64]
- Create a table of contents.[65]
- Give the receiving party an estimate of discovery volume.[66]
- Identify any third-party ESI according to which device it came from.[67]
- Produce third-party ESI in the format it was received or in a reasonably usable format.[68]
- Produce discoverable materials generated by a party during its investigation in a searchable and reasonably usable format.[69]
- Produce a cover letter to accompany e-discovery that describes the number of media, the unique identifiers of the media, a brief description of the contents including a table of contents if created, and any Bates ranges or other unique production identifiers.[70]

Receiving Party
- Inspect e-discovery promptly after its receipt and give notice to the producing party of any production issues or problems that may impede using the e-discovery.[7]

---

64. ESI Protoco , Recommendations ¶ 6.
65. ESI Protoco , Strategies ¶ 5(b).
66. ESI Protoco , Strategies ¶ 5(h).
67. ESI Protoco , Strategies ¶ 5( ).
68. ESI Protoco , Strategies ¶ 6(g).
69. ESI Protoco , Strategies ¶ 6(h).
70. ESI Protoco , Strategies ¶ 7(c).
71. ESI Protoco , Strategies ¶ 5(o).

Appendix B
ESI Protocol

Appendix B: ESI Protocol

Recommendations for Electronically Stored Information (ESI) Discovery Production in Federal Criminal Cases

Department of Justice (DOJ) and Administrative Office of the U.S. Courts (AO) Joint Electronic Technology Working Group (JETWG)

February 2012

Appendix B: ESI Protocol

Introduction to Recommendations for ESI Discovery in Federal Criminal Cases

Today, most information is created and stored electronically. The advent of electronically stored information (ESI) presents an opportunity for greater efficiency and cost savings for the entire criminal justice system, which is especially important for the representation of indigent defendants. To realize those benefits and to avoid undue cost, disruption, and delay, criminal practitioners must educate themselves and employ best practices for managing ESI discovery.

The Joint Electronic Technology Working Group JETWG) was created to address best practices for the efficient and cost-effective management of post-indictment ESI discovery between the government and defendants charged in federal criminal cases. JETWG was established in 1998 by the director of the Administrative Office of the U.S. Courts (AOUSC) and the Attorney General of the United States. It consists of representatives of the Administrative Office of the U.S. Courts, Defender Services Office (DSO), the Department of Justice (DOJ), Federal Public and Community Defender Organizations (FPDOs and CDOs), private attorneys who accept Criminal Justice Act (CJA) appointments, and liaisons from the United States judiciary and other AOUSC offices.

JETWG has prepared recommendations for managing ESI discovery in federal criminal cases, which are contained in the following three documents:

1. **Recommendations for ESI Discovery in Federal Criminal Cases.** The Recommendations provide the general framework for managing ESI, including planning, production, transmission, dispute resolution, and security.

2. **Strategies and Commentary on ESI Discovery in Federal Criminal Cases.** The Strategies provide technical and more particularized guidance for implementing the recommendations, including definitions of terms. The Strategies will evolve in light of changing technology and experience.

3. **ESI Discovery Checklist.** A one-page checklist for addressing ESI production issues.

Criminal e Discovery

The Recommendations, Strategies, and Checklist are intended for cases where the volume and/or nature of the ESI produced as discovery significantly increases the complexity of the case. They are not intended for all cases. The Recommendations, Strategies, and Checklist build upon the following basic principles:

Principle 1: Lawyers have a responsibility to have an adequate understanding of electronic discovery. (See #4 of the Recommendations.)

Principle 2: In the process of planning, producing, and resolving disputes about ESI discovery, the parties should include individuals with sufficient technical knowledge and experience regarding ESI. (See #4 of the Recommendations.)

Principle 3: At the outset of a case, the parties should meet and confer about the nature, volume, and mechanics of producing ESI discovery. Where the ESI discovery is particularly complex or produced on a rolling basis, an ongoing dialogue may be helpful. (See #5 of the Recommendations and Strategies.)

Principle 4: The parties should discuss what formats of production are possible and appropriate and what formats can be generated. Any format selected for producing discovery should maintain the ESI's integrity, allow for reasonable usability, reasonably limit costs, and, if possible, conform to industry standards for the format. (See #6 of the Recommendations and Strategies.)

Principle 5: When producing ESI discovery, a party should not be required to take on substantial additional processing or format-conversion costs and burdens beyond what the party has already done or would do for its own case preparation or discovery production. (See #6 of the Recommendations and Strategies.)

Principle 6: Following the meet-and-confer, the parties should notify the court of ESI discovery production issues or problems that they reasonably anticipate will significantly affect the handling of the case. (See #5(s) of the Strategies.)

Appendix B: ESI Protocol

Principle 7: The parties should discuss ESI discovery transmission methods and media that promote efficiency, security, and reduced costs. The producing party should provide a general description and maintain a record of what was transmitted. (See #7 of the Recommendations and Strategies.)

Principle 8: In multidefendant cases, the defendants should authorize one or more counsel to act as the discovery coordinator(s) or seek the appointment of a Coordinating Discovery Attorney. (See #8 of the Recommendations and Strategies.)

Principle 9: The parties should make good faith efforts to discuss and resolve disputes over ESI discovery, involving those with the requisite technical knowledge when necessary, and they should consult with a supervisor, or obtain supervisory authorization, before seeking judicial resolution of an ESI discovery dispute or alleging misconduct, abuse, or neglect concerning the production of ESI. (See #9 of the Recommendations.)

Principle 10: All parties should limit dissemination of ESI discovery to members of their litigation team who need, and are approved for, access, and they should also take reasonable and appropriate measures to secure ESI discovery against unauthorized access or disclosure. (See #10 of the Recommendations.)

The Recommendations, Strategies, and Checklist set forth a collaborative approach to ESI discovery involving mutual and interdependent responsibilities. The goal is to benefit all parties by making ESI discovery more efficient and secure, and less costly.

Criminal e Discovery

Recommendations for ESI Discovery Production in Federal Criminal Cases

1. Purpose

These Recommendations are intended to promote the efficient and cost-effective post-indictment production of electronically stored information (ESI) in discovery[72] between the government and defendants charged in federal criminal cases and to reduce unnecessary conflict and litigation over ESI discovery by encouraging the parties to communicate about ESI discovery issues, by creating a predictable framework for ESI discovery and by establishing methods for resolving ESI discovery disputes without the need for court intervention.

ESI discovery production involves the balancing of several goals:

a) The parties must comply with their legal discovery obligations;

b) the volume of ESI in many cases may make it impossible for counsel to personally review every potentially discoverable item, and, as a consequence, the parties increasingly will employ software tools for discovery review, so ESI discovery should be done in a manner to facilitate electronic search, retrieval, sorting, and management of discovery information;

c) the parties should look for ways to avoid unnecessary duplication of time and expense for both parties in the handling and use of ESI;

d) subject to subparagraph (e), below, the producing party should produce its ESI discovery materials in industry-standard formats;

---

72. The Recommendations and Strategies are intended to app y on y to disc o-sure of ESI under Federa Ru es of Crimina Procedure 16 and 26.2, *Brady*, *Giglio*, and the Jencks Act, and they do not app y to, nor do they create any rights, privi eg-es, or benefits during, the gathering of ESI as part of the parties' crimina or civi investigations. The ega princip es, standards, and practices app icab e to the discovery phase of crimina cases serve different purposes than those app icab e to crimina and civi investigations.

Appendix B: ESI Protocol

e) the producing party is not obligated to undertake additional processing desired by the receiving party that is not part of the producing party's own case preparation or discovery production[73]; and

f) the parties must protect their work product, privileged, and other protected information.

The following Recommendations are a general framework for informed discussions between the parties about ESI discovery issues. The efficient and cost-effective production of ESI discovery materials is enhanced when the parties communicate early and regularly about any ESI discovery issues in their case, and when they give the court notice of ESI discovery issues that will significantly affect the handling of the case.

2. Scope: Cases Involving Significant ESI

No single approach to ESI discovery is suited to all cases. These Recommendations are intended for cases where the volume and/or nature of the ESI produced as discovery significantly increases the complexity of the case.[74] In simple or routine cases, the parties should provide discovery in the manner they deem most efficient in accordance with the Federal Rules of Criminal Procedure, local rules, and custom and practice within their district.

Due to the evolving role of ESI in criminal cases, these Recommendations and the parties' practices will change with technology and experience. As managing ESI discovery becomes more routine, it is anticipated that the parties will develop standard processes for ESI discovery that become the accepted norm.

---

73. One examp e of the producing party undertaking additiona processing for its discovery production is a oad fi e that enab es the receiving party to oad discovery materia s into its software.

74. Courts and itigants wi continue to seek ways to identify cases deserving specia consideration. Whi e the facts and circumstances of cases wi vary, some factors may inc ude: (1) a arge vo ume of ESI; (2) unique ESI issues, inc uding native fi e formats, vo uminous third-party records, nonstandard and proprietary software formats; and/or (3) mu tip e-defendant cases accompanied by a significant vo ume of ESI.

3. Limitations

These Recommendations and the accompanying Strategies do not alter the parties' discovery obligations or protections under the U.S. Constitution, the Federal Rules of Criminal Procedure, the Jencks Act, or other federal statutes, case law, or local rules. They may not serve as a basis for allegations of misconduct or claims for relief, and they do not create any rights or privileges for any party.

4. Technical Knowledge and Experience

For complex ESI productions, each party should involve individuals with sufficient technical knowledge and experience to understand, communicate about, and plan for the orderly exchange of ESI discovery. Lawyers have a responsibility to have an adequate understanding of electronic discovery.

5. Planning for ESI Discovery Production—The Meet-and-Confer Process

At the outset of a case involving substantial or complex ESI discovery, the parties should meet and confer about the nature, volume, and mechanics of producing ESI discovery. The parties should determine how to ensure that any meet-and-confer process does not run afoul of speedy trial deadlines. Where the ESI discovery is particularly complex or produced on a rolling basis, an ongoing dialogue during the discovery phase may be helpful. In cases where it is authorized, providing ESI discovery to an incarcerated defendant presents challenges that should be discussed early. Also, cases involving classified information will not fit within the Recommendations and Strategies due to the unique legal procedures applicable to those cases. ESI that is contraband (*e.g.*, child pornography) requires special discovery procedures. The Strategies and Checklist provide detailed recommendations on planning for ESI discovery.

Appendix B: ESI Protocol

6. Production of ESI Discovery

Production of ESI discovery involves varied considerations depending upon the ESI's source, nature, and format. Unlike certain civil cases, in criminal cases the parties generally are not the original custodian or source of the ESI they produce in discovery. The ESI gathered by the parties during their investigations may be affected or limited by many factors, including the original custodian's or source's information technology systems, data management practices, and resources; the party's understanding of the case at the time of collection; and other factors. Likewise, the electronic formats used by the parties for producing ESI discovery may be affected or limited by several factors, including the source of the ESI; the format(s) in which the ESI was originally obtained; and the party's legal discovery obligations, which may vary with the nature of the material. The Strategies and Checklist provide detailed recommendations on production of ESI discovery.

General recommendations for the production of ESI discovery are as follows:

    a.   The parties should discuss what formats of production are possible and appropriate and what formats can be generated. Any format selected for producing discovery should, if possible, conform to industry standards for the format.[75]

    b.   ESI received from third parties should be produced in the format(s) it was received or in reasonably usable format(s). ESI from the government's or defendant's business records should be produced in the format(s) in which it was maintained or in reasonably usable format(s).

    c.   Discoverable ESI generated by the government or defense during the course of their investigations (*e.g.,* investigative reports, witness interviews, demonstrative exhibits, etc.) may be handled differently than in 6(a) and (b) above be-

---

[75]. An example of a format of production might be the production of TIFF images, OCR text files, and load files created for a specific software application. Another format of production would be native-file production, which would accommodate files with unique issues, such as spreadsheets with formulas and databases. ESI in a particular case might warrant more than one format of production depending upon the nature of the ESI.

cause the parties' legal discovery obligations and practices vary according to the nature of the material, the applicable law, evolving legal standards, the parties' policies, and the parties' evolving technological capabilities.

d. When producing ESI discovery, a party should not be required to take on substantial additional processing or format-conversion costs and burdens beyond what the party has already done or would do for its own case preparation or discovery production. For example, the producing party need not convert ESI from one format to another or undertake additional processing of ESI beyond what is required to satisfy its legal disclosure obligations. If the receiving party desires ESI in a condition different from what the producing party intends to produce, the parties should discuss what is reasonable in terms of expense and mechanics, who will bear the burden of any additional cost or work, and how to protect the producing party's work product or privileged information. Nonetheless, with the understanding that in certain instances the results of processing ESI may constitute work product not subject to discovery, these recommendations operate on the general principle that where a producing party elects to engage in processing of ESI, the results of that processing should, unless they constitute work product, be produced in discovery along with the underlying ESI so as to save the receiving party the expense of replicating the work.

7. Transmitting ESI Discovery

The parties should discuss transmission methods and media that promote efficiency, security, and reduced costs. In conjunction with ESI transmission, the producing party should provide a general description and maintain a record of what was transmitted. Any media should be clearly labeled. The Strategies and Checklist contain detailed recommendations on transmission of ESI discovery, including the potential use of email to transmit ESI.

Appendix B: ESI Protocol

8. Coordinating Discovery Attorney

In cases involving multiple defendants, the defendants should authorize one or more counsel to act as the discovery coordinator(s), or seek the appointment of a Coordinating Discovery Attorney,[76] and authorize that person to accept, on behalf of all defense counsel, the ESI discovery produced by the government. Generally, the format of production should be the same for all defendants, but the parties should be sensitive to different needs and interests in multiple-defendant cases.

9. Informal Resolution of ESI Discovery Matters

a. Before filing any motion addressing an ESI discovery issue, the moving party should confer with opposing counsel in a good-faith effort to resolve the dispute. If resolution of the dispute requires technical knowledge, the parties should involve individuals with sufficient knowledge to understand the technical issues, clearly communicate the problem(s) leading to the dispute, and either implement a proposed resolution or explain why a proposed resolution will not solve the dispute.

b. The Discovery Coordinator within each U.S. Attorney's Office should be consulted in cases presenting substantial issues or disputes.

c. To avoid unnecessary litigation, prosecutors and Federal Defender Offices[77] should institute procedures that re-

---

76. Coordinating Discovery Attorneys (CDAs) are AOUSC-contracted attorneys who have technological knowledge and experience, resources, and staff to effectively manage complex ESI in multiple-defendant cases. The CDAs may be appointed by the court to provide in-depth and significant hands-on assistance to CJA panel attorneys and FDO staff in selected multiple-defendant cases that require technology and document management assistance. They can serve as a primary point of contact for the U.S. Attorney's Office to discuss ESI production issues for all defendants, resulting in lower overall case costs for the parties. If a panel attorney or FDO is interested in utilizing the services of the CDA, they should contact the National Litigation Support Administrator or Assistant National Litigation Support Administrator for the Office of Defender Services at 510-637-3500.

77. For private attorneys appointed under the Criminal Justice Act, this subsection (c) is not applicable.

quire line prosecutors and defenders (1) to consult with a supervisory attorney before filing a motion seeking judicial resolution of an ESI discovery dispute, and (2) to obtain authorization from a supervisory attorney before suggesting in a pleading that opposing counsel has engaged in any misconduct, abuse, or neglect concerning production of ESI.

d. Any motion addressing a discovery dispute concerning ESI production should include a statement of counsel for the moving party relating that after consultation with the attorney for the opposing party, the parties have been unable to resolve the dispute without court action.

10. Security: Protecting Sensitive ESI Discovery from Unauthorized Access or Disclosure

Criminal case discovery entails certain responsibilities for all parties in the careful handling of a variety of sensitive information, for example, grand jury material, the defendant's records, witness identifying information, information about informants, information subject to court protective orders, confidential personal or business information, and privileged information. With ESI discovery, those responsibilities are increased because ESI is easily reproduced and disseminated, and unauthorized access or disclosure could, in certain circumstances, endanger witness safety; adversely affect national security or homeland security; leak information to adverse parties in civil suits; compromise privacy, trade secrets, or classified, tax return, or proprietary information; or prejudice the fair administration of justice. The parties' willingness to produce early, accessible, and usable ESI discovery will be enhanced by safeguards that protect sensitive information from unauthorized access or disclosure.

All parties should limit dissemination of ESI discovery to members of their litigation team who need, and are approved for, access. They should also take reasonable and appropriate measures to secure ESI discovery against unauthorized access or disclosure.

During the initial meet-and-confer and before ESI discovery is produced, the parties should discuss whether there is confidential, pri-

Appendix B: ESI Protocol

vate, or sensitive information in any ESI discovery they will be providing. If such information will be disclosed, then the parties should discuss how the recipients will prevent unauthorized access to, or disclosure of, that ESI discovery, and, absent agreement on appropriate security, the producing party should seek a protective order from the court addressing management of the particular ESI at issue. The producing party has the burden to raise the issue anew if it has concerns about any ESI discovery it will provide in subsequent productions. The parties may choose to have standing agreements so that their practices for managing ESI discovery are not discussed in each case. The Strategies contain additional guidance in sections 5(f), 5 p), and 7(e).

Criminal e Discovery

Strategies and Commentary on ESI Discovery in Federal Criminal Cases

1. Purpose

This commentary contains strategies for implementing the ESI discovery Recommendations and specific technical guidance. Over time it will be modified in light of experience and changing technology. Definitions of common ESI terms are provided in paragraph 11, below.

2. Scope of ESI Gathered

In order to promote efficiency and avoid unnecessary costs, when gathering ESI, the parties should take into consideration the nature, volume, and mechanics of managing ESI.

3. Limitations

Nothing contained herein creates any rights or privileges for any party.

4. Technical Knowledge and Experience

No additional commentary.

5. Planning for e-Discovery Production—The Meet-and-Confer Process

To promote efficient ESI discovery, the parties may find it useful to discuss the following:
    a. **ESI discovery produced.** The parties should discuss the ESI being produced according to the following general categories:
        i. *Investigative materials* (investigative reports, surveillance records, criminal histories, etc.)
        ii. *Witness statements* (interview reports, transcripts of prior testimony, Jencks statements, etc.)

Appendix B: ESI Protocol

    iii. *Documentation of tangible objects* (*e.g.*, records of seized items or forensic samples, search warrant returns, etc.)

    iv. *Third parties' ESI digital devices* (computers, phones, hard drives, thumb drives, CDs, DVDs, cloud computing, etc., including forensic images)

    v. *Photographs and video/audio recordings* (crime scene photos; photos of contraband, guns, money; surveillance recordings; surreptitious monitoring recordings; etc.)

    vi. *Third party records and materials* (including those seized, subpoenaed, and voluntarily disclosed)

    vii. *Title III wiretap information* (audio recordings, transcripts, line sheets, call reports, court documents, etc.)

    viii. *Court records* (affidavits, applications, and related documentation for search and arrest warrants, etc.)

    ix. *Tests and examinations*

    x. *Experts* (reports and related information)

    xi. *Immunity agreements, plea agreements, and similar materials*

    xii. *Discovery materials with special production considerations* (such as child pornography, trade secrets, tax return information, etc.)

    xiii. *Related matters* (state or local investigative materials, parallel proceedings materials, etc.)

    xiv. *Discovery materials available for inspection but not produced digitally*

    xv. *Other information*

b. **Table of contents.** If the producing party has not created a table of contents prior to commencing ESI discovery production, it should consider creating one describing the general categories of information available as ESI discovery. In complex discovery cases, a table of contents to the available discovery materials can help expedite the opposing party's review of discovery, promote early settlement, and avoid discovery disputes, unnecessary expense, and undue delay.[78] Because no single table of contents is appropriate for every case, the producing party may devise a table of contents that is suited to the materials it provides in discovery, its resources, and other considerations.[79]

c. **Forms of production.** The producing party should consider how discoverable materials were provided to it or maintained by the source (*e.g.*, paper or electronic), whether it has converted any materials to a digital format that can be used by the opposing party without disclosing the producing party's work product, and how those factors may affect the production of discovery materials in electronic formats. For particularized guidance see paragraph 6, below. The parties should be flexible in their application of the concept of "maintained by the source." The goals are to retain the ESI's integrity, to allow for reasonable usability, and to reasonably limit costs.[80]

d. **Proprietary or legacy data.** Special consideration should be given to data stored in proprietary or legacy sys-

---

78. *See, e.g.*, *U.S. v. Skilling*, 554 F.3d 529, 577 (5th Cir. 2009) (no *Brady* vio ation where government disc osed severa -hundred-mi ion-page database with searchab e fi es and produced set of hot documents and indices).

79. A tab e of contents is intended to be a genera , high- eve guide to the categories of ESI discovery. Because a tab e of contents may not be detai ed, comp ete, or free of errors, the parties sti have the responsibi ity to review the ESI discovery produced. With ESI, particu ar content usua y can be ocated using avai ab e e ectronic search too s. There are many ways to construct a genera tab e of contents. For examp e, a tab e of contents cou d be a fo der structure as set forth above in paragraph 2(a)(i xv), where ike items are p aced into fo ders.

80. For examp e, when the producing party processes ESI to app y Bates numbers, oad it into itigation software, create TIFF images, etc., the ESI is s ight y modified and no onger in its origina state. Simi ar y, some modification of the ESI may be necessary and proper in order to a ow the parties to protect privi eged information, and the processing and production of ESI in certain formats may resu t in the oss or a teration of some metadata that is not significant in the circumstances of the particu ar case.

Appendix B: ESI Protocol

tems, for example, video surveillance recordings in an uncommon format, proprietary databases, or software that is no longer supported by the vendor. The parties should discuss whether a suitable generic-output format or report is available. If a generic output is not available, the parties should discuss the specific requirements necessary to access the data in its original format.

e. **Attorney–client, work product, and protected information issues.**[8] The parties should discuss whether there is privileged, work product, or other protected information in third-party ESI or their own discoverable ESI and should discuss proposed methods and procedures for segregating such information and resolving any disputes.[82]

f. **Confidential and personal information.** The parties should identify and discuss the types of confidential or personal information present in the ESI discovery, appropriate security for that information, and the need for any protective orders or redactions. See also section 5 p) below.

g. **Incarcerated defendant.** If the defendant is incarcerated and the court or correctional institution has authorized discovery access in the custodial setting, the parties should consider what institutional requirements or limitations may affect the defendant's access to ESI discovery, such as limitations on hardware or software use.[83]

h. **ESI discovery volume.** To assist in estimating the receiving party's discovery costs and to the extent that the producing party knows the volume of discovery materials

---

81. Attorney c ient and work-product issues (*see, e.g.,* F. R. Crim. P. 16(a)(2) and (b)(2)) arising from the parties' own case preparation are beyond the scope of these Recommendations, and they need not be part of the meet-and-confer discussion.

82. If third-party records are subject to an agreement or court order invo ving a se ective waiver of attorney c ient or work-product privi eges (see F.R.E. 502), then the parties shou d discuss how to hand e those materia s.

83. Because pretria detainees often are he d in oca jai s (for space, protective custody, cost, or other reasons), which have varying resources and security needs, there are no uniform practices or ru es for pretria detainees' access to ESI discovery. Reso ution of the issues associated with such access is beyond the scope of the Recommendations and Strategies.

it intends to produce immediately or in the future, the producing party may provide such information if such disclosure would not compromise the producing party's interests. Examples of volume include the number of pages of electronic images of paper-based discovery, the volume (*e.g.*, gigabytes) of ESI, the number and aggregate length of any audio or video recordings, and the number and volume of digital devices. Disclosures concerning expected volume are not intended to be so detailed as to require a party to disclose what it intends to produce as discovery before it has a legal obligation to produce the particular discovery material (*e.g.*, Jencks material). Similarly, the parties' estimates are not binding and may not serve as the basis for allegations of misconduct or claims for relief.

i. **Naming conventions and logistics.** The parties should, from the outset of a case, employ naming conventions that would make the production of discovery more efficient. For example, in a Title III wiretap case generally it is preferable that the naming conventions for the audio files, the monitoring logs, and the call transcripts be consistent so that it is easy to cross-reference the audio calls with the corresponding monitoring logs and transcripts. If at the outset of discovery production a naming convention has not yet been established, the parties should discuss a naming convention before the discovery is produced. The parties should discuss logistics and the sharing of costs or tasks that will enhance ESI production.

j. **Paper materials.** For options and particularized guidance on paper materials see paragraphs 6(a) and (e), below.

k. **Any software and hardware limitations.** As technology continues to evolve, the parties may have software and hardware constraints on how they can review ESI. Any limitations should be addressed during the meet-and-confer.

l. **ESI from seized or searched third-party ESI digital devices.** When a party produces ESI from a seized or searched third-party digital device (*e.g.*, computer, cell

Appendix B: ESI Protocol

phone, hard drive, thumb drive, CD, DVD, cloud computing, or file share), the producing party should identify the digital device that held the ESI, and, to the extent that the producing party already knows, provide some indication of the device's probable owner or custodian and the location where the device was seized or searched. Where the producing party only has limited authority to search the digital device (*e.g.*, limits set by a search warrant's terms), the parties should discuss the need for protective orders or other mechanisms to regulate the receiving party's access to or inspection of the device.

m. **Inspection of hard drives and/or forensic (mirror) images.** Any forensic examination of a hard drive, whether it is an examination of a hard drive itself or an examination of a forensic image of a hard drive, requires specialized software and expertise. A simple copy of the forensic image may not be sufficient to access the information stored, as specialized software may be needed. The parties should consider how to manage inspection of a hard drive and/or production of a forensic image of a hard drive and what software and expertise will be needed to access the information.

n. **Metadata in third-party ESI.** If a producing party has already extracted metadata from third-party ESI, the parties should discuss whether the producing party should produce the extracted metadata together with an industry-standard load file or, alternatively, produce the files as received by the producing party from the third party.[84] Neither party need undertake additional processing beyond its own case preparation, and both parties are entitled to protect their work product and privileged or other protected information. Because the term "metadata" can encompass different categories of information, the parties should clearly describe what categories of metadata are

---

84. The producing party is, of course, imited to what it received from the third party. The third party's processing of the information can affect or imit what metadata is avai ab e.

being discussed, what the producing party has agreed to produce, and any known problems or gaps in the metadata received from third parties.

o. **A reasonable schedule for producing and reviewing ESI.** Because ESI involves complex technical issues, two stages should be addressed. First, the producing party should transmit its ESI in sufficient time to permit reasonable management and review. Second, the receiving party should be proactive about testing the accessibility of the ESI production *when it is received*. Thus, a schedule should include a date for the receiving party to notify the producing party of any production issues or problems that are impeding use of the ESI discovery.

p. **ESI security.** During the first meet-and-confer, the parties should discuss ESI discovery security and, if necessary, the need for protective orders to prevent unauthorized access to, or disclosure of, ESI discovery that any party intends to share with team members via the Internet or similar system, including:

   i. what discovery material will be produced that is confidential, private, or sensitive, including, but not limited to, grand jury material, witness identifying information, information about informants, a defendant's or co-defendant's personal or business information, information subject to court protective orders, confidential personal or business information, or privileged information;

   ii. whether encryption or other security measures during transmission of ESI discovery are warranted;[85]

   iii. what steps will be taken to ensure that only authorized persons have access to the electronically stored or disseminated discovery materials;

---

85. The parties shou d consu t their itigation support personne concerning encryption or other security options.

Appendix B: ESI Protocol

    iv.   what steps will be taken to ensure the security of any website or other electronic repository against unauthorized access;

    v.   what steps will be taken at the conclusion of the case to remove discovery materials from a website or similar repository; and

    vi.   what steps will be taken at the conclusion of the case to remove or return ESI discovery materials from the recipient's information system(s), or to securely archive them to prevent unauthorized access.

Note: Because all parties want to ensure that ESI discovery is secure, the Department of Justice, Federal Defender Offices, and CJA counsel are compiling an evolving list of security concerns and recommended best practices for appropriately securing discovery. Prosecutors and defense counsel with security concerns should direct inquiries to their respective ESI liaisons,[86] who, in turn, will work with their counterparts to develop best practice guidance.

q.   **Other issues.** The parties should address other issues they can anticipate, such as protective orders, "claw-back" agreements[87] between the government and criminal defendant(s), or any issues related to the preservation or collection of ESI discovery.

r.   **Memorializing agreements.** The parties should memorialize any agreements reached to help forestall later disputes.

---

86. Federa Defender Organizations and CJA pane attorneys shou d contact Sean Broderick (Nationa Litigation Support Administrator) or Ke y Scribner (Assistant Nationa Litigation Support Administrator) at 510-637-3500, or by emai : sean broderick@fd.org, ke y scribner@fd.org. Prosecutors shou d contact Andrew Go dsmith (Nationa Crimina Discovery Coordinator) at Andrew.Go dsmith@usdoj.gov or John Haried (Assistant Nationa Crimina Discovery Coordinator) at John.Haried@usdoj.gov.

87. A "c aw-back" agreement out ines procedures to be fo owed to protect against waiver of privi ege or work-product protection due to inadvertent production of documents or data.

s. **Notice to court.**

    i. *Preparing for the meet and confer.* A defendant who anticipates the need for technical assistance to conduct the meet-and-confer should give the court adequate advance notice if it will be filing an ex parte funds request for technical assistance.

    ii. *Following the meet and confer.* The parties should notify the court of ESI discovery production issues or problems that they anticipate will significantly affect when ESI discovery will be produced to the receiving party, when the receiving party will complete its accessibility assessment of the ESI discovery received,[88] whether the receiving party will need to make a request for supplemental funds to manage ESI discovery, or the scheduling of pretrial motions or trial.

6. **Production of ESI Discovery**

    a. **Paper Materials.** Materials received in paper form may be produced in that form,[89] made available for inspection, or, if they have already been converted to digital format, produced as electronic files that can be viewed and searched. Methods are described below in paragraph 6(b).

    b. **Electronic production of paper documents.** Three possible methodologies:

        i. *Single page TIFFs.* Production in TIFF and OCR format consists of the following three elements:

            (1) Paper documents are scanned to a picture or image that produces one file per page. Documents should be unitized. Each elec-

---

88. *See* paragraph 5(o) of the Strategies, above.
89. The decision whether to scan paper documents requires striking a ba ance between resources (inc uding personne and cost) and efficiency. The parties shou d make that determination on a case-by-case basis.

Appendix B: ESI Protocol

      tronic image should be stamped with a unique page label or Bates number.

    (2) Text from that original document is generated by OCR and stored in separate text files without formatting in a generic format using the same file naming convention and organization as image file.

    (3) Load files that tie together the images and text.

  ii. *Multi page TIFFS.* Production in TIFF and OCR format consists of the following two elements:

    (1) Paper documents are scanned to a picture or image that produces one file per document. Each file may have multiple pages. Each page of the electronic image should be stamped with a unique page label or Bates number.

    (2) Text from that original document is generated by OCR and stored in separate text files without formatting in a generic format using the same file naming convention and organization as the image file.

  iii. *PDF.* Production in multi-page, searchable PDF format consists of the following one element:

    (1) Paper documents scanned to a PDF file with text generated by OCR included in the same file. This produces one file per document. Documents should be unitized. Each page of the PDF should be stamped with a unique Bates number.

  iv. *Note re: color documents.* Paper documents should not be scanned in color unless the color content of an individual document is particularly significant to the case.[90]

c. **ESI production.** Three possible methodologies:

　i. *Native files as received.* Production in a native file format without any processing consists of a copy of ESI files in the same condition as they were received.

　ii. *ESI converted to electronic image.* Production of ESI into a TIFF or PDF and extracted text format consists of the following four elements:

　　(1) Electronic documents converted from their native format into a picture/image. The electronic image files should be computer-generated, as opposed to printed and then imaged. Each electronic image should be stamped with a unique Bates number.

　　(2) Text from that original document is extracted or pulled out and stored without formatting in a generic format.

　　(3) Metadata (*i.e.*, information about that electronic document), depending upon the type of file converted and the tools or methodology used, that has been extracted and stored in an industry-standard format. The metadata must include information about structural relationships between documents, *e.g.*, parent–child relationships.

　　(4) Load files that tie together the images, text, and metadata.

---

90. Co or scanning substantia y s ows the scanning process and creates huge e ectronic fi es, which consume storage space, making the storage and transmission of information difficu t. An origina signature, handwritten margina ia in b ue or red ink, and co ored text high ights are examp es of co or content that may be particu- ar y significant to the case.

Appendix B: ESI Protocol

    iii. *Native files with metadata.* Production of ESI in a processed native-file format consists of the following four elements:

        (1) The native files.

        (2) Text from that original document is extracted or pulled out and stored without formatting in a generic format.

        (3) Metadata (*i.e.*, information about that electronic document), depending upon the type of file converted and the tools or methodology used, that has been extracted and stored in an industry-standard format. The metadata must include information about structural relationships between documents, *e.g.*, parent–child relationships.

        (4) Load files that tie together the native file, text, and metadata.

d. **Forensic images of digital media.** Forensic images of digital media should be produced in an industry-standard forensic format, accompanied by notice of the format used.

e. **Printing ESI to paper.** The producing party should not print ESI (including TIFF images or PDF files) to paper as a substitute for production of the ESI unless agreed to by the parties.

f. **Preservation of ESI materials received from third parties**. A party receiving potentially discoverable ESI from a third party should, to the extent practicable, retain a copy of the ESI as it was originally produced in case it is subsequently needed to perform quality control or verification of what was produced.

g. **Production of ESI from third parties.** ESI from third parties may have been received in a variety of formats, for example, in its original format (native, such as Excel or Word), as an image (TIFF or PDF), as an image with searchable text (TIFF or PDF with OCR text), or as a combination of any of these. The third party's format can affect or limit the available options for production as well as what associated information (metadata) might be available. ESI received from third parties should be produced in the format(s) it was received or in reasonably usable format(s). ESI received from a party's own business records should be produced in the format(s) in which it was maintained or in reasonably usable form(s). The parties should explore what formats of production[9] are possible and appropriate and discuss what formats can be generated. Any format selected for producing discovery should, if possible and appropriate, conform to industry standards for the format.

h. **ESI generated by the government or defense.** Paragraphs 6(f) and 6(g) do not apply to discoverable materials generated by the government or defense during the course of their investigations (*e.g.*, demonstrative exhibits, investigative reports and witness interviews—see subparagraph i, below, etc.) because the parties' legal discovery obligations and practices vary according to the nature of the material, the applicable law, evolving legal standards, and the parties' evolving technological capabilities. Thus, such materials may be produced differently from third-party ESI. However, to the extent practicable, this material should be produced in a searchable and reasonably usable format. Parties should consult with their investigators in advance of preparing discovery to ascertain the investigators' ESI capabilities and limitations.

i. **Investigative reports and witness interviews.** Investigative reports and witness interviews may be produced in paper form if they were received in paper form or if the final version is in paper form. Alternatively, they may be produced as electronic images (TIFF images or PDF files),

---

91. An examp e of a format of production might be the production of TIFF images, OCR text fi es, and oad fi es created for a specific software app ication. Another format of production wou d be native-fi e production, which wou d accommodate fi es with unique issues, such as spreadsheets with formu as and databases.

Appendix B: ESI Protocol

particularly when needed to accommodate any necessary redactions. Absent particular issues such as redactions or substantial costs or burdens of additional processing, electronic versions of investigative reports and witness interviews should be produced in a searchable text format (such as ASCII text, OCR text, or plain text (.txt)) in order to avoid the expense of reprocessing the files. To the extent possible, the electronic image files of investigative reports and witness interviews should be computer-generated (as opposed to printed to paper and then imaged) in order to produce a higher-quality, searchable text, which will enable the files to be more easily searched and more cost-effectively utilized.[92]

j. **Redactions**. ESI and/or images produced should identify the extent of redacted material and its location within the document.

k. **Photographs and video and audio recordings**. A party producing photographs or video or audio recordings that either were originally created using digital devices or have previously been digitized should disclose the digital copies of the images or recordings if they are in the producing party's possession, custody or control. When technically feasible and cost-efficient, photographs and video and audio recordings that are not already in a digital format should be digitized into an industry-standard format if and when they are duplicated. The producing party is not required to convert materials obtained in analog format to digital format for discovery.

l. **Test runs.** Before producing ESI discovery, a party should consider providing samples of the production format for a test run and, once a format is agreed upon, produce all ESI discovery in that format.

---

92. For guidance on making computer-generated versions of investigative reports and witness interview reports, see the description of production of TIFF, PDF, and extracted text formats in paragraphs 6(b)(ii)(1) and (ii).

m. **Access to originals.** If the producing party has converted paper materials to digital files, converted materials with color content to black and white images, or processed audio, video, or other materials for investigation or discovery, it should provide reasonable access to the originals for inspection and/or reprocessing.

7. **Transmitting ESI Discovery**

   a. ESI discovery should be transmitted on electronic media of sufficient size to hold the entire production, for example, a CD, DVD, or thumb drive.[93] If the size of the production warrants a large-capacity hard drive, then the producing party may require the receiving party to bear the cost of the hard drive and to satisfy requirements for the hard drive that are necessary to protect the producing party's IT system from viruses or other harm.

   b. The media should be clearly labeled with the case name and number, the producing party, a unique identifier for the media, and a production date.

   c. A cover letter should accompany each transmission of ESI discovery providing basic information, including the number of media, the unique identifiers of the media, a brief description of the contents (including a table of contents if created), any applicable bates ranges or other unique production identifiers, and any necessary passwords to access the content. Passwords should not be in the cover letter accompanying the data, but in a separate communication.

   d. The producing party should retain a write-protected copy of all transmitted ESI as a preserved record to resolve any subsequent disputes.

---

93. Ro ing productions may, of course, use mu tip e media. The producing party shou d avoid using mu tip e media when a sing e media wi faci itate the receiving party's use of the materia .

Appendix B: ESI Protocol

e. **Email transmission.** When considering transmission of ESI discovery by email, the parties' obligation varies according to the sensitivity of the material, the risk of harm from unauthorized disclosure, and the relative security of email versus alternative transmission. The parties should consider three categories of security:

　　i. *Not appropriate for email transmission*: Certain categories of ESI discovery are never appropriate for email transmission, including, but not limited to, certain grand jury materials; materials affecting witness safety; materials containing classified, national security, homeland security, tax return, or trade secret information; or similar items.

　　ii. *Encrypted email transmission*: Certain categories of ESI discovery warrant encryption or other secure transmission due to their sensitive nature. The parties should discuss and identify those categories in their case. This would ordinarily include, but not be limited to, information about informants, confidential business or personal information, and information subject to court protective orders.

　　iii. *Unencrypted email transmission*: Other categories of ESI discovery not addressed above may be appropriate for email transmission, but the parties always need to be mindful of their ethical obligations.[94]

8. Coordinating Discovery Attorney

Coordinating Discovery Attorneys (CDAs) are AOUSC-contracted attorneys who have technological knowledge and experience, resources, and staff to effectively manage complex ESI in multiple-defendant

---

94. I ustrative of the security issues in the attorney c ient context are ABA Op. 11-459 (Duty to Protect the Confidentia ity of E-mai Communications with One's C ient) and ABA Op. 99-413 (Protecting the Confidentia ity of Unencrypted E-Mai).

cases. The CDAs may be appointed by the court to provide additional in-depth and significant hands-on assistance to CJA panel attorneys and FDO staff in selected multiple-defendant cases that require technology and document-management assistance. They can serve as a primary point of contact for the U.S. Attorney's Office to discuss ESI production issues for all defendants, resulting in lower overall case costs for the parties. If you have any questions regarding the services of a CDA, please contact either Sean Broderick (National Litigation Support Administrator) or Kelly Scribner (Assistant National Litigation Support Administrator) at 510-637-3500, or by email: sean broderick@fd.org, kelly scribner@fd.org.

9.   Informal Resolution of ESI Discovery Matters

No additional commentary.

10.   Security: Protecting Sensitive ESI Discovery from Unauthorized Access or Disclosure

See sections 5(f) (Confidential and personal information), 5(p) (ESI security), and 7(e) (Email transmission) of the Strategies for additional guidance.

11.   Definitions

To clearly communicate about ESI, it is important that the parties use ESI terms in the same way. Below are common ESI terms used when discussing ESI discovery:

   a.   **Cloud computing.** With cloud computing, the user accesses a remote computer hosted by a cloud service provider over the Internet or an intranet to access software programs or create, save, or retrieve data, for example, to send messages or create documents, spreadsheets, or databases. Examples of cloud computing include Gmail, Hotmail, Yahoo! Mail, Facebook, and online banking.

   b.   **Coordinating Discovery Attorney (CDA).** An AOUSC-contracted attorney who has technological know-

Appendix B: ESI Protocol

ledge and experience, resources, and staff to effectively manage complex ESI in multiple-defendant cases, and who may be appointed by a court in selected multiple-defendant cases to assist CJA panel attorneys and/or FDO staff with discovery management.

c. **Document unitization.** Document unitization is the process of determining where a document begins (its first page) and ends (its last page), with the goal of accurately describing what was a "unit" as it was received by the party or was kept in the ordinary course of business by the document's custodian. A "unit" includes attachments—for example, an email with an attached spreadsheet. Physical unitization utilizes actual objects such as staples, paper clips, and folders to determine pages that belong together as documents. Logical unitization is the process of human review of each individual page in an image collection using logical cues to determine pages that belong together as documents. Such cues can be consecutive page numbering, report titles, similar headers and footers, and other logical cues.

d. **ESI (Electronically Stored Information).** Any information created, stored, or utilized with digital technology. Examples include, but are not limited to, word-processing files, e-mail and text messages (including attachments); voicemail; information accessed via the Internet, including social networking sites; information stored on cell phones; information stored on computers, computer systems, thumb drives, flash drives, CDs, tapes, and other digital media.

e. **Extracted text.** The text of a native file extracted during ESI processing of the native file, most commonly when native files are converted to TIFF format. Extracted text is more accurate than text created by the OCR processing of document images that were created by scanning and will therefore provide higher quality search results.

f. **Forensic image (mirror image) of a hard drive or other storage device.** A process that preserves the entire contents of a hard drive or other storage device by creating a bit-by-bit copy of the original data without altering the original media. A forensic examination or analysis of an imaged hard drive requires specialized software and expertise to both create and read the image. User created files, such as email and other electronic documents, can be extracted, and a more complete analysis of the hard drive can be performed to find deleted files and/or access information. A forensic or mirror image is not a physical duplicate of the original drive or device; instead it is a file or set of files that contains all of the data bits from the source device. Thus a forensic or mirror image cannot simply be opened and viewed as if you were looking at the original device. Indeed, forensic or mirror images of multiple hard drives or other storage devices can be stored on a single hard drive of sufficient capacity.

g. **Image of a document or document image.** An electronic "picture" of how the document would look if printed. Images can be stored in various file formats, the most common of which are TIFFs and PDFs. Document images, such as TIFFs and PDFs, can be created directly from native files or created by scanning hard copy.

h. **Load file.** A cross-reference file used to import images or data into databases. A data load file may contain Bates numbers, metadata, paths to native files, coded data, and extracted or OCR text. An image load file may contain document boundary, image type, and path information. Load files must be obtained and provided in software-specific formats to ensure they can be used by the receiving party.

i. **Metadata.** Data that describes characteristics of ESI, for example, the author, date created, and date last accessed of a word processing document. Metadata is generally not reproduced in full form when a document is printed to paper or electronic image. Metadata can describe how, when and by whom ESI was created, accessed, modified, formatted, or collected. Metadata can be supplied by applications, users, or the file system, and it can be altered

Appendix B: ESI Protocol

       intentionally or inadvertently. Certain metadata can be extracted when native files are processed for litigation. Metadata is found in different places and in different forms. Some metadata, such as file dates and sizes, can easily be accessed by users; other metadata can be hidden or embedded and unavailable to computer users who are not technically adept. Note that some metadata may be lost or changed when an electronic copy of a file is made using ordinary file-copy methods.

j. **Native file.** A file as it was created in its native software, for example a Word, Excel, or PowerPoint file, or an email in Outlook or Lotus Notes.

k. **OCR (Optical Character Recognition).** A process that converts a picture of text into searchable text. The quality of the created text can vary greatly depending on the quality of the original document, the quality of the scanned image, the accuracy of the recognition software, and the quality control process of the provider. Generally speaking, OCR does not handle handwritten text or text in graphics well. OCR conversion rates can range from 50–98% accuracy depending on the underlying document. A full page of text is estimated to contain 2,000 characters, so OCR software with even 90% accuracy would create a page of text with approximately 200 errors.

l. **Parent–child relationships.** Related documents are described as having a parent–child relationship, for example, where the email is the parent and an attached spreadsheet is the child.

m. **PDF (Portable Document Format).** A file format created by Adobe that allows a range of options, including electronic transmission, viewing, and searching.

n. **TIFF (Tagged Image File Format).** An industry-standard file format for storing scanned and other digital black-and-white, grey-scale, and full-color images.

Criminal e Discovery

ESI Discovery Production Checklist

- ☐ Is this a case where the volume or nature of ESI significantly increases the case's complexity?
- ☐ Does this case involve classified information?
- ☐ Does this case involve trade secrets, or national security or homeland security information?
- ☐ Do the parties have appropriate technical advisors to assist?
- ☐ Have the parties met and conferred about ESI issues?
- ☐ Have the parties addressed the format of ESI being produced? Categories may include:
    - ☐ Investigative reports and materials
    - ☐ Witness statements
    - ☐ Tangible objects
    - ☐ Third-party ESI digital devices (computers, phones, etc.)
    - ☐ Photos, video and audio recordings
    - ☐ Third-party records
    - ☐ Title III wiretap information
    - ☐ Court records
    - ☐ Tests and examinations
    - ☐ Experts
    - ☐ Immunity and plea agreements
    - ☐ Discovery materials with special production considerations
    - ☐ Related matters
    - ☐ Discovery materials available for inspection but not produced digitally
    - ☐ Other information
- ☐ Have the parties addressed ESI issues involving:
    - ☐ Table of contents?
    - ☐ Production of paper records as either paper or ESI?
    - ☐ Proprietary or legacy data?
    - ☐ Attorney–client, work-product, or other privilege issues?
    - ☐ Sensitive confidential, personal, grand jury, classified, tax return, trade secret, or similar information?

Appendix B: ESI Protocol

- ☐ Whether email transmission is inappropriate for any categories of ESI discovery?
- ☐ Incarcerated defendant's access to discovery materials?
- ☐ ESI discovery volume for receiving party's planning purposes?
- ☐ Parties' software or hardware limitations?
- ☐ Production of ESI from third-party digital devices?
- ☐ Forensic images of ESI digital devices?
- ☐ Metadata in third-party ESI?
- ☐ Redactions?
- ☐ Reasonable schedule for producing party?
- ☐ Reasonable schedule for receiving party to give notice of issues?
- ☐ Appropriate security measures during transmission of ESI discovery, e.g., encryption?
- ☐ Adequate security measures to protect sensitive ESI against unauthorized access or disclosure?
- ☐ Need for protective orders, claw-back agreements, or similar orders or agreements?
- ☐ Collaboration on sharing costs or tasks?
- ☐ Need for receiving party's access to original ESI?
- ☐ Preserving a record of discovery produced?

☐ Have the parties memorialized their agreements and disagreements?
☐ Do the parties have a system for resolving disputes informally?
☐ Is there a need for a designated discovery coordinator for multiple defendants?
☐ Do the parties have a plan for managing/returning ESI at the conclusion of the case?

Appendix C
First Appearance e-Discovery Colloquy

Appendix C: First Appearance e Discovery Colloquy

At the first appearance of a defendant and after appointment of counsel, engage parties in the following colloquy concerning e-discovery.

A. Ask the **prosecutor** about possible e-discovery in the case, and generally how the government will proceed:

1. Does the government intend to produce any discovery in electronic formats?
2. Does the volume or nature of the government's electronic discovery significantly increase the complexity of the case?
3. Are you familiar with the ESI Protocol?
4. Are you going to utilize the ESI Protocol?

B. Ask **defense counsel** about familiarity with managing e-discovery, and generally how the defense will proceed:

1. Are you familiar with the ESI Protocol?
2. Do you have a copy of the ESI Protocol to rely on as you work through the e-discovery? If not, the government can provide a copy.
3. What is your experience with complex e-discovery cases?
4. Are you familiar with various software products and e-discovery services that can be used to review and organize e-discovery? Have you used them before?
5. Have you worked with litigation support, paralegals, or IT staff before to review e-discovery?
6. Do you presently have litigation support, paralegals, or IT staff who can work with you to review and organize electronic evidence? If not, you may need to decide what type of expert or experts you will need. Do you know how to do that?

C. Engage **both parties** in a discussion of how they will cooperatively address complex e-discovery:
   1. Are you utilizing the ESI Protocol?
   2. Have you already had a meet-and-confer to address e-discovery issues? If so, do you have any agreements or a discovery plan? If not, what is your plan for addressing e-discovery issues?
   3. Will the volume or nature of the e-discovery potentially affect:
      a. Speedy trial deadlines for this case?
      b. Scheduling pretrial motions?
      c. Scheduling trial?

D. Address **all attorneys** about what the court expects of them in managing a complex e-discovery criminal case:
   1. I expect you already have, or will promptly gain, an adequate understanding of and adequate technical assistance in e-discovery matters.
   2. I expect the lawyers on this case to manage electronic discovery effectively, efficiently, and responsibly, and to seek cost savings.
   3. I also expect the lawyers on this case to determine what software programs and expert assistance you need to review the discovery. If you do not know what type of expert to retain or what software programs to use, you should consult with someone knowledgeable about e-discovery before making those decisions.
   4. While the lawyers may, and should, employ litigation support, paralegals, and/or IT staff, ultimately, the *lawyers* are responsible for e-discovery decisions made in this case.
   5. I encourage all parties to utilize a collaborative approach to e-discovery based upon the mutual

Appendix C: First Appearance e Discovery Colloquy

and interdependent responsibilities of the opposing parties. The ESI Protocol offers a model of such an approach.

6. An important part of the process is a meet-and-confer discussion about the e-discovery issues in this case. I encourage you to use the checklist at the end of the ESI Protocol during your meet-and-confer session. For scheduling purposes, some of the key steps to pay attention to are:

   a. The parties should discuss a reasonable e-discovery production schedule.

   b. Defense counsel should be proactive about testing the accessibility of the e-discovery production when it is received, and promptly notify the government of any problems in accessing the materials.

   c. If defense counsel determines that additional funds for expert assistance are needed, that needs to be brought to the court's attention promptly.

7. I expect that the parties will promptly notify the court of any e-discovery issues that might reasonably affect speedy trial deadlines, or the scheduling of pretrial motions or trial.

E. If there are **CJA attorneys** appointed to defend one or more defendants, address funding issues with them:

   1. If you will be hiring expert assistance to organize and review the e-discovery, have them help you decide on a realistic estimation of the time that they will need to do so. If that exceeds the expert's costs "cap," file an ex parte, sealed motion asking to exceed the capped amount, explaining the work that would be done and how you or they arrived at that cost estimate.

Criminal e Discovery

F. If there are multiple defendants (so multiple defense counsel) in the case, the advisability of coordinating e-discovery among defendants should be raised at the first appearance. This gives counsel time to discuss and decide potential coordination before a meet-and-confer session.

   1. I am *not* ordering you to do this, but you may want to consider whether to designate one defense attorney to manage e-discovery.

G. Advise **defense counsel** about the availability of resources to help guide them in managing complex e-discovery:

   1. If you need advice and guidance about getting started, there are resources available to help you decide how to productively get the information you need from the e-discovery. The National Litigation Support Team, part of the Defender Services Office (DSO) of the Administrative Office of the U.S. Courts,[95] is available to provide guidance about how to efficiently, and cost-effectively, manage e-discovery. If you are not familiar with the technology and expert assistance you will need, you should contact them right away, well before the meet-and-confer session. They can also tell you about contracts they have secured for reduced prices on some of the software programs that may help you review and organize the evidence.

   2. Another resource available to defender offices and CJA counsel is appointment of a coordinating discovery attorney. Those handling voluminous or complex e-discovery (especially when there are multiple defendants) can have an attorney expert in e-discovery appointed to work with defense counsel to help coordinate, organize, and process e-discovery. After exploring the nature and vol-

---

[95] The Nationa Litigation Support Team can be contacted at (510) 637-3500.

Appendix C: First Appearance e Discovery Colloquy

ume of e-discovery, and what it will take for defense counsel to review it, if you think this case needs a coordinating discovery attorney appointed, then file an ex parte sealed motion explaining why, and the court will consider it.

H. Finally, the court may decide to set a discovery status conference (giving parties enough time to secure expert assistance if needed, and to hold a meaningful meet-and-confer session) to verify that e-discovery is moving smoothly, cooperatively, and effectively. Inform **all parties**:

1. I am going to schedule a discovery status conference to follow up on the progress the parties are making with the e-discovery, and ensure that any problems with it are resolved early.

2. I encourage you to conduct your meet-and-confer session well before the discovery status conference so that you can address and resolve any issues.

Appendix D
Discovery Status Conference e-Discovery Colloquy

Appendix D: Discovery Status Conference e Discovery Colloquy

Having already addressed e-discovery issues at the first appearance, the court may schedule a discovery status conference to confirm whether e-discovery is being addressed by parties intelligently, efficiently, and cost-effectively. At a discovery status conference, engage parties in the following colloquy concerning the status of their e-discovery.

A. In cases with multiple defendants, the court would have asked parties to consider whether one defense attorney should be responsible for receiving, distributing, and possibly coordinating work on e-discovery for all defense teams. The court can follow up on that by asking **all multiple-defense counsel**:

    1. Is this a case where management of the e-discovery would benefit from having either:

        a. A single defense attorney receiving e-discovery from the government for all defendants and being responsible for disseminating it to all defendants; or

        b. A coordinating discovery attorney appointed by the court?

    2. If one of you will manage the discovery for all defendants, have you already selected that attorney? If you want to use a coordinating discovery attorney, have you contacted the National Litigation Support Team to ensure that doing so is appropriate for this case?

B. The court can then check on the parties' success in trying to decide and resolve e-discovery issues. To that end, it should address **both parties**:

    1. Did the parties conduct a meet-and-confer session?

    2. Did you utilize the ESI Protocol?

    3. Did you have litigation support specialists (if needed) to help you decide how to manage the ESI dis-

covery? Did you have your litigation support specialists with you at the meet-and-confer session?

    4.   Were the parties able to reach decisions as to when, how, and in what format the e-discovery will be produced?

    5.   Were the parties able to reach decisions on other e-discovery issues (such as those listed in the checklist of the ESI Protocol)?

C.   Verify with the **government** whether there is an e-discovery production schedule agreed upon:

    1.   Do you have an e-discovery production schedule?

        a.   What is it?

        b.   Have you started producing e-discovery to the defense?

        c.   Do you anticipate a "rolling" production of e-discovery?

D.   The court can also verify with the defense whether it has performed an initial review of any disclosures to ascertain that it can access and utilize the ESI. Then the court should inquire of **defense counsel** whether the defense has an e-discovery production schedule that was agreed upon:

    1.   Do you have a schedule as to when you will do a summary initial review of the e-discovery (to ascertain that you can open and use it as produced)?

        a.   What is it?

        b.   If production has started, have you performed a review of the e-discovery to verify that you can access and use it?

    2.   You may have e-discovery to disclose to the government. Did you already discuss any defense e-discovery in the meet-and-confer session?

    3.   Do you have an e-discovery production schedule?

Appendix D: Discovery Status Conference e Discovery Colloquy

        a.   What is it?

        b.   Have you started producing e-discovery to the government?

        c.   Do you anticipate a "rolling" production of discovery?

E.   If the parties did not accomplish all that was necessary, the court may want to reiterate to all parties some of its advisements about expectations and resources from the First Appearance e-Discovery Colloquy, sections D–G, contained in Appendix C.

F.   The court may decide to inquire about any unresolved discovery issues or disputes. If so, it could ask **both parties**:

        1.   Were all e-discovery issues resolved by the meet-and-confer session? Were there any e-discovery issues that were not resolved?

G.   If there are unresolved issues, the court may want to set another discovery status conference to settle those matters.

The Federal Judicial Center

Board
The Chief Justice of the United States, Chair
Judge Catherine C. Blake, U.S. District Court for the District of Maryland
Judge Curtis L. Collier, U.S. District Court for the Eastern District of Tennessee
Magistrate Judge Jonathan W. Feldman, U.S. District Court for the Western District of New York
Judge Kent A. Jordan, U.S. Court of Appeals for the Third Circuit
Judge Michael J. Melloy, U.S. Court of Appeals for the Eighth Circuit
Judge Kimberly J. Mueller, U.S. District Court for the Eastern District of California
Chief Judge C. Ray Mullins, U.S. Bankruptcy Court for the Northern District of Georgia
James C. Duff, Director of the Administrative Office of the U.S. Courts

Director
Judge Jeremy D. Fogel

Deputy Director
John S. Cooke

About the Federal Judicial Center
The Federal Judicial Center is the research and education agency of the federal judicial system. It was established by Congress in 1967 (28 U.S.C. §§ 620–629), on the recommendation of the Judicial Conference of the United States.

By statute, the Chief Justice of the United States chairs the Center's Board, which also includes the director of the Administrative Office of the U.S. Courts and seven judges elected by the Judicial Conference.

The organization of the Center reflects its primary statutory mandates. The Education Division plans and produces education and training for judges and court staff, including in-person programs, video programs, publications, curriculum packages for in-district training, and Web-based programs and resources. The Research Division examines and evaluates current and alternative federal court practices and policies. This research assists Judicial Conference committees, who request most Center research, in developing policy recommendations. The Center's research also contributes substantially to its educational programs. The Federal Judicial History Office helps courts and others study and preserve federal judicial history. The International Judicial Relations Office provides information to judicial and legal officials from foreign countries and informs federal judicial personnel of developments in international law and other court systems that may affect their work. Two units of the Director's Office—the Information Technology Office and the Editorial & Information Services Office—support Center missions through technology, editorial and design assistance, and organization and dissemination of Center resources.

www.ingramcontent.com/pod-product-compliance
Lightning Source LLC
Chambersburg PA
CBHW060405190526
45169CB00002B/755